I0119770

Canada Dept. of Militia and Defence

Statement Showing the Names of all Veterans who Have Proved their Rights to Partake in the Grant of $50,000 Voted Last session By Parliament ...

Canada Dept. of Militia and Defence

Statement Showing the Names of all Veterans who Have Proved their Rights to Partake in the Grant of $50,000 Voted Last session By Parliament ...

ISBN/EAN: 9783337156077

Printed in Europe, USA, Canada, Australia, Japan

Cover: Foto ©Andreas Hilbeck / pixelio.de

More available books at **www.hansebooks.com**

MILITIA PENSIONS.

WAR OF 1812-15.

DEPARTMENT OF MILITIA AND DEFENCE.

RETURN FOR 1876-77.

STATEMENT

SHOWING THE NAMES OF ALL VETERANS WHO HAVE PROVED THEIR RIGHTS TO
PARTAKE IN THE GRANT OF $50,000 VOTED LAST SESSION BY PARLIAMENT
IN FAVOR OF MILITIAMEN OF 1812-15, AND THE ACTION TAKEN IN
EACH CASE DURING THE CURRENT FINANCIAL YEAR;
ALSO THE NAMES OF ALL THOSE WHO HAVE
APPLIED FOR A PENSION AND UPON
WHOSE CASES NO DECISION
HAS BEEN GIVEN.

Printed by Order of Parliament.

OTTAWA:
PRINTED BY MACLEAN, ROGER & CO., WELLINGTON STREET
1877.

RETURN

To an ORDER of the HOUSE OF COMMONS, dated 5th March, 1~77;.—For a
Return showing the names of all Veterans who have proved their
right to participate in the grant of $50,000, voted last session by Parlia-
ment in favor of Militiamen of 1812 and 1815, and the action taken in
each case during the current financial year.

By Command,

R. W. SCOTT,
Secretary of State.

DEPARTMENT OF THE SECRETARY OF STATE,
OTTAWA, 8th March, 1877.

———

PENSIONS TO MILITIAMEN OF 1812-15.

PROVINCE OF ONTARIO.

Electoral District.	Post Office.	Number of Case.	Name of Militiaman.	Amount Paid.	Remarks.
				$ cts.	
ADDINGTON	Arden	2446	Wood, William	20 00	
	do	2447	Woodcock, Abraham	20 00	
	Bell Rock	1913	Piercy, Michael	20 00	
	Centreville	606	Rombough, Jacob	20 00	
	Colebrook	200	Habcock, Peter	20 00	
	do	202	Loughlen, Jacob	20 00	
	do	611	Neddo, John	20 00	
	Desert Lake	679	Waller, Hudson	20 00	
	Enterprise	1202	Hawley, Sylas	20 00	
	Harrowsmith	1595	Ward, Lewis	20 00	
	do	1647	Babcock, Samuel	20 00	
	Harthington	796	Vanluven, John	20 00	
	Loughborough	797	Clement, Lewis	20 00	
	do	2233	Dawson, John	20 00	
	Moscow	199	Card, Amos	20 00	
	do	523	Card, Stephen	20 00	
	do	526	Card, John	20 00	
	do	524	Clark, Robert	30 00	
	do	525	Huffman, Elijah	20 00	
	do	1960	Vanvolkenburg, Paul	20 00	
	Newburg	798	Shuller, Conrad	20 00	
	do	3453	Shutter, Andrew		Services not proved.
	Parkham	3131	Veley, Aaron H	20 00	
	Petworth	1107	Vanest, James	20 00	
	Verona	680	Snider, John B		
	Wilmur	1644	Orser, Isaac	20 00	Dead.
	do	1646	Strope, Christopher	20 00	
	Yarker	201	Scott, Samuel	20 00	
	do	1851	Shibley, Henry		Dead.

PENSIONS TO MILITIAMEN OF 1812-15.—*Continued.*

PROVINCE OF ONTARIO.—*Continued.*

Electoral District.	Post Office.	Number of Case.	Name of Militiaman.	Amount Paid.	Remarks.
				$ cts.	
ALGOMA	Bruce Mines	3473	Rol, Joseph		Services not proved.
	Manitowaning	3190	Assiginack, Amable	20 00	
	do	3196	Bemanackaning, M	20 00	
	Sault Ste. Marie	3206	Lafond, Joseph	20 00	
	do	3207	Mastat, Raymond	20 00	
	do	3240	Thibault, Pierre	20 00	
BOTHWELL	Ullin	3276	Causley, Solomon	20 00	
	Clearville	447	Burns, David	20 00	
	do	34	McDonell, Peter	20 00	
	Dawn Mills	1562	Phillips, John	20 00	
	do	2248	Devens, Abraham		Services not proved.
	Dresden	3056	Sager, John	20 00	
	Florence	3015	Quakenbush, Isaac	20 00	
	do	1845	Laird, George	20 00	
	Morpeth	35	Goff, Alexander	20 00	
	do	36	Green, Freeman	20 00	
	Palmyra	33	Eberle, Henry	20 00	
	do	37	Armstrong, Charles	20 00	
	Sombra	328	Kennedy, Morris	20 00	
BRANT	Thamesville	2358	Stevens, Richard		Dead.
	Brantford	1782	Buck, Peter	20 00	
	do	2932	Lowrey, Ephraim	20 00	
	Burford	1773	Perley, C. Strange	20 00	
	Cainsville	309	Corson, Robert	20 00	
	do	2301	Files, Malchi		Dead.
	Harley	1658	Lester, Henry		Dead.
	Harrisburg	1908	Vanevery, Charles	20 00	
	Langford	1783	Oles, John	20 00	
	do	1189	Strowbridge, Benjamin	20 00	

PENSIONS TO MILITIAMEN OF 1812-15.—*Continued.*

PROVINCE OF ONTARIO.—*Continued.*

Electoral District.	Post Office.	Number of Case.	Name of Militiaman.	Amount Paid.	Remarks
				$ cts.	
BRANT.—*Continued*	Mohawk., ...	2099	McAllster, Robert.........		No return.
	do	1187	Secord, Asa................	20 00	
	do	1812	Sturges, John M	20 00	
	Mount Vernon......	1868	Landon, Stephen	20 00	
	Oakland	2419	Beacham, John.............	20 00	
	do	1418	Chambers, John	20 00	
	do	1424	Petrie, John........	20 00	
	Paris	1195	Cassadu, James............		Dead.
	do	2816	Wilson, Ebenezer........	20 00	
	Scotland	1788	Freeland, Daniel A......	20 00	
	do	57	Petit, Charles..............	20 00	
	do	1102	Beamer, Philip	2. .	
	St. George............	698	Bonham, Josuah... ..	00	
	do	3007	Crandell, Laban		Services not proved.
	Tuscarora............	3170	Fraser, Joseph...... ...		
	do	3171	Givens, James...............		
	do	3169	Silversmith, Henry.......	20 00	
	do	3172	Tutlee, John	20 00	
	do	3173	Winey, Jacob	20 00	
	do	2836	Johnson, John S.	20 00	
	do	3174	Johnson, William	20 00	
BROCKVILLE	Addison	2479	Lewis, Ira..........	20 00	
	Brockville	3077	Beaupré, Peter		Dead.
	do	2327	McNish, Joseph	20 00	
	do	283	McEatborn, John.........		Dead.
	do	2263	Beach, Enos.	20 00	
	do	2671	Clow, Henry..............		Dead.
	do	2693	Hunter, James	20 00	
	do	2652	Rorison, James....	20 00	

PENSIONS TO MILITIAMEN OF 1812–15.—*Continued.*

PROVINCE OF ONTARIO.—*Continued.*

Electoral District.	Post Office.	Number of Case.	Name of Militiaman.	Amount Paid.	Remarks.
				$ cts.	
BROCKVILLE.—*Con*	Brockville..........	1052	Wright, Amos............	....	Dead.
	do	2657	Campbell, James..........	20 00	
	do	2873	Mead, Curtis	....	Services not proved.
	Greenbush	2261	Shipman, Daniel	20 00	
	Lyn	1624	Howard, Mathew..	20 00	
	do	80	Mott, Reu! ?	20 00	
	do	365	McLean, William..........	20 00	
	do	2085	Pennock, Aaron..........	....	Dead.
	do	893	Purvis, George..........	20 00	
	do	68	Whitenarsh, David . ..	20 00	
	do	3326	Hayes, John C..........	20 00	
BRUCE	Kincardine	3423	Donovan, Samuel..........	....	Services not proved.
	North Bruce	2170	Rawn, Jacob......	20 00	
	Sargeen..............	3072	Madwashmind, John	20 00	
	Teeswater	3424	Fulford, Jonathan..........	....	Services not proved.
CARDWELL..........	Caledon	1575	Vanloyck, Gilbert..........	....	No return.
	do	2218	Malloy, Hugh	20 00	
	Longwood	3464	Caldwel, William	....	Services not proved.
CORNWALL..........	Eamer's Corner.....	3141	Gordon, Ross	20 00	
	Harrison Corner....	1702	McNaughton, John	20 00	
	do ...	1034	Eamer, Michael	20 00	
	Mille Roches	2355	Martin, Frank.............	20 00	
	Northfield	2457	Cryderman, William......	20 00	
	St. Andrews West.	2366	Chisholm, John	20 00	
	do ...	1011	Campbell, Donald........	20 00	
	do ...	3058	McDonald, Donald	20 00	
	do ...	3097	McDonell, James...	....	No return
	do ...	998	McDonell, Angus	20 00	
	do ...	3448	McDonnell, Angus	....	Services not proved.

7

Electoral District.	Post Office.	Number of Case.	Name of Militiaman.	Amount Paid.	Remarks.
				$ cts.	
CORNWALL.—*Con.*	Cornwall	1009	Eastman, Nadab	20 00	
	do	1007	Groves, James	20 00	
	do	2456	Loney, John	20 00	
	do	999	McDonald, Ronald	20 00	
	do	1000	McDonald, James	20 00	
	do	1002	McDouuell, Donald	20 00	
	do	1012	McDonald, Angus	20 00	
	do	2852	McDonald, Lachlin	20 00	
	do	995	McDonell, Alexander	20 00	
	do	996	McDonell, Allen		Dead.
	do	1003	McDonell, Allen	20 00	
	do	997	McMillan, Donald	20 00	
	do	1001	McPhail, Donald	20 00	
	do	1679	Meyers, Godfrey	20 00	
	do	2634	Silsmer, Philip	20 00	
	do	3188	McDonald, Alexander	20 00	
	do	265	Robidoux, Joseph		Dead.
	do	3070	Tyo, Francis	20 00	
CARLETON	Fitzroy Harbour	1405	Landon, John	20 00	
	do	2256	McLeod, Duncan	20 00	
	Kars	227	Eastman, David	20 00	
	do	1675	Eastman, John		No return
	Ottawa	1013	Berichon, Isaac	20 00	
	do	458	Danis, Honoré	20 00	
	do	3109	Delage, Julien	20 00	
	do	2869	Delage, Pierre		Dead.
	do	2689	Leduc, Etienne	20 00	
	do	1683	Mallet, Joseph	20 00	
	do	1678	McGee, Francis	20 00	

PENSIONS TO MILITIAMEN OF 1812-15.—*Continued.*

PROVINCE OF ONTARIO.—*Continued.*

Electoral District.	Post Office.	Number of Case.	Name of Militiaman.	Amount Paid.	Remarks.
				$ cts.	
CARLETON.—*Con.*	Ottawa	438	Ossant, Pierre	20 00	
	do	2631	Rodrigue, John	20 00	
	do	3122	Cousineau, Louis	20 00	
	do	3412	Chesley, S. J		Services not proved.
	North Gower	395	McEwen, William	20 00	
	Rochesterville	2336	Lalande, Hyacinthe	20 00	
DUNDAS	Bourk's Hill	1029	Bedstead, Francis	20 00	
	Brinston's Corner	493	Bush, William	20 00	
	do	492	Collison, John	20 00	
	do	494	Lock, John	20 00	
	do	1273	Strailer, Henry	20 00	
	do	1100	Campbell, William	20 00	
	Dixon's Corner	491	Haines, Jacob	20 00	
	do	501	Lock, James	20 00	
	do	1272	Vansteenburg, Francis		Dead.
	Dunbar	2027	Barkeley, Everet	20 00	
	do	1040	Barkeley, Martin	20 00	
	do	1020	Bedstead, Alexander	20 00	
	do	1032	Miller, Henry	20 00	
	Hoasic	1019	Fetterly, George	20 00	
	Inkerman	593	Elbare, John	20 00	
	do	592	Knight, Charles	20 00	
	do	914	Landon, James	20 00	
	do	590	Slater, James	20 00	
	do	591	Vancamp, John	20 00	
	Iroquois	486	Carman, Jacob	20 00	
	do	1394	Carman, Mathew	20 00	
	do	485	Coons, Samuel	20 00	
	do	490	Hartle, Mathew	20 00	

PENSIONS TO MILITIAMEN OF 1812-15.—*Continued.*

PROVINCE OF ONTARIO.—*Continued.*

Electoral District.	Post Office.	Number of Case.	Name of Militiaman.	Amount Paid.	Remarks.
				$ cts.	
DUNDAS.—*Con*	Iroquois	498	Keck, Isaac	20 00	
	do	495	Kirtner, Conrad	20 00	
	do	484	Toussant, Ennis	20 00	
	do	499	Turner, John C	20 00	
	do	500	Shaver, Henry	20 00	
	do	487	Strader, John	20 00	
	do	496	Shaver, Michael	20 00	
	do	489	Shaver, John	20 00	
	do	2656	Thompson, Jesse	20 00	
	do	1613	Steenburg, John	20 00	
	Morrisburg	126	Brouse, Peter	20 00	
	do	56	De Castle, Carlo	20 00	
	do	1026	Fravts, John	20 00	
	do	1033	Miller, John	20 00	
	do	587	Mosley, Lucius		Left limits.
	do	1027	Munro, John	20 00	
	do	2854	Scott, William		Dead.
	do	1021	Sullivan, Michael	20 00	
	do	297	Casselman, John T	20 00	
	do	727	Weageant, Jacob		Services not proved.
	Morewood	912	Crowder, Andrew	20 00	
	do	911	Schwerfizer, G. Fred	20 00	
	North Williamsb'g.	1025	Cook, John	20 00	
	do	1680	Empey, Christopher	20 00	
	do	2003	Garlough, Jacob	20 00	
	do	345	Loucks, John W	20 00	
	do	1030	Loucks, William	20 00	
	do	1023	Hanes, John	20 00	
	South Mountain	1506	Shaver, William	20 00	

PENSIONS TO MILITIAMEN OF 1812-15.—*Continued.*

PROVINCE OF ONTARIO.—*Continued.*

Electoral District.	Post Office.	Number of Case.	Name of Militiaman.	Amount Paid.	Remarks.
				$ cts.	
DUNDAS.—*Con*	Smirleville	588	Loucks, Jacob	20 00	
	Winchester	218	Casselman, William		Dead.
	do	2943	Hawn, Henry		Dead.
	Winchest'r Springs	1028	Barragar, Jacob	20 00	
	do	589	Shaver, William	20 00	
	do	497	Shaver, James	20 00	
	West Winchester	915	Barragar, Andrew	20 00	
	do	916	Mallory, Joseph		No return.
	do	913	Redmond, Marcus	20 00	
DURHAM	Bowmanville	1759	Trull, John C	20 00	
	do	1758	Vancamp, Jesse	20 00	
	Dale	2729	Vandervoort, David	20 00	
	Orono	1927	Jones, Eldad	20 00	
	Port Hope	836	Chisholm, Angus		No return.
	do	403	Harris, Myndert	20 00	
	do	329	Herrlman, Luther	20 00	
ESSEX	Amherstburg	3045	Clark, Alexander		Dead.
	do	207	Robidoux, Jean B	20 00	
	Belle River	272	Buisson, Pierre	20 00	
	do	1313	Knapp, Colbert		Dead.
	Canard River	663	Bondy, Charles		No return.
	do	1518	Drouillard, Basile	20 00	
	do	1519	Vigneux, Louis	20 00	
	Colchester	815	Aikman, Alexander	20 00	
	do	705	Lypps, Henry	20 00	
	do	704	Marantelle, Antoine	20 00	
	do	370	Ferris, Isaac	20 00	
	Harrow	3091	Pennock, Nathaniel	20 00	
	do	2209	Ferris, John	20 00	

PENSIONS TO MILITIAMEN OF 1812-15.—*Continued.*

PROVINCE OF ONTARIO.—*Continued.*

Electoral District.	Post Office.	Number of Case.	Name of Militiamen.	Amount Paid.	Remarks.
				$ cts.	
ESSEX – *Con*	Kingsville	20	Harris, Samuel............	20 00	
	do	2730	Toffelmire, John...........	20 00	
	Leamington.........	700	Brown, Henry...............	20 00	
	do	1810	Lane, Isaac...............	20 00	
	do	1213	McCarthy, Charles........	20 00	
	North Ridge.........	619	Clark, John...............	20 00	
	Oxley	206	White, David	20 00	
	Ryegate	1912	Benoit, Pierre............	20 00	
	do	1521	Souliere, François........		No return.
	Ruthven.............	1959	Sears, James H............	20 00	
	do	1856	Stockwell, John...........	20 00	
	Sandwich...........	2095	Ivon, Joseph	20 00	
	do	861	Laughton, John B.........	20 00	
	do	3001	Souliere, Jean B..........	20 00	
	Stony Point	662	Mailloux, Antoine........		No return.
	Trudell	2915	Labonté Francis..........	20 00	
	Windsor.............	3002	Gauthier, Jacques........	20 00	
	do	1011	Merantelle, Benjamin....	20 00	
	do	1508	Parent, Isaac............	20 00	
	do	3113	Suider, James............		Services not proved
....	Alboro...............	1508	McDonald, Peter.........	20 00	
	Avon...............	2743	Allen, Aaron	20 00	
	Aylmer	2741	Bradley, Onesime........	20 00	
	do	3022	Rychman, John	20 00	
	do	2714	Harper, Samuel	20 00	
	do	2768	House, Mathew...........	20 00	
	do	3018	House, Frederick.........	20 00	
	do	2302	Phelps, Othniel		Left limits.
	Bayham	2384	Laur, John	20 00	

PENSIONS TO MILITIAMEN OF 1812-15.—*Continued.*

PROVINCE OF ONTARIO.—*Continued.*

Electoral District.	Post Office.	Number of Case.	Name of Militiaman.	Amount Paid.	Remarks.
				$ cts.	
ELGIN.—*Con*........	Eden	168	Howie, Samuel.....:......	20 00	
	Fingal	135	McQueen, James...........	20 00	
	do	197	Stafford, Ralph.............	20 00	
	do	137	Wilson, Benjamin S......	20 00	
	Groveend	2345	Franklln, Horatio N......	20 00	
	do	2789	Hawkinson, Thomas......	....	Dead.
	Kingswill...	2793	Vancisse, Joseph...........	20 00	
	Frome....................	853	Sharron, Hugh.............	20 00	
	Luton	3017	Ostrander, Thadeus	20 00	
	Lyons	3465	Kelly, Nathan	....	Services not proved.
	New Sarum...........	965	Boughmer, Mathias.......	20 00	
	do	123	Oakes, Garret	....	No return.
	Port Bruce...........	2830	Barr, Henry....................	20 00	
	do	3016	Hunter, Socrates..........	....	Service not proved.
	Port Burwell........	1467	Cameron, George W......	20 00	
	do	1308	Eakins, Robert.............	20 00	
	do	2130	McDormand, Thomas.....	20 00	
	do	1309	Ricoard, Francois...........	....	Services not proved.
	do	2129	McDermund, Thomas.....	20 00	
	do	3471	Scealey, Anthony	....	Services, not proved.
	Springfield............	2950	Rossignol, Antolne........	20 00	
	Straffordville........	165	Griffin, David..............	20 00	
	do	1710	Hause, James	20 00	
	St. Thomas...........	2012	Dexter, Ransom	20 00	
	do	3025	Learn, John...................	20 00	
	do	1677	Smuck, Peter	20 00	
	do	852	Stringer, Henry.............	20 00	
	do	4	St. Etienne, Jean..	20 00	
	Talbotville	855	Berdon, Jacob...............	20 00	
	Southwould	1956	Wood, Philo	....	Dead.

PENSIONS TO MILITIAMEN OF 1812–15.—*Continued.*

PROVINCE OF ONTARIO.—*Continued.*

Electoral District.	Post Office.	Number of Case.	Name of Militiaman.	Amount Paid.	Remarks.
				$ cts.	
ELGIN.—*Continued.*	Union	376	Donn, Jno. Thompson...	20 00	
	Vienna	167	Yocum, George	20 00	
	Yarmouth Centre.	2192	Caugbell, George	20 00	
	do	1691	Couse, John	20 00	
FRONTENAC	Battersea	694	Randall, Benjamin		Dead.
	do	170	Vanluven, Henry	20 00	
	Bedford	3155	Jones, Stephen	20 00	
	Elginburgh	3271	Snook, Tunis	20 00	
	do	1870	Purdy, Jesse	20 00	
	Glenvale	2527	Ellerbeck, James	20 00	
	Pittsferry	2871	Root, Daniel	20 00	
	Wolf Island	1767	Bennett, Alvah	20 00	
GLENGARRY	do	2052	Mosier, Nicholas	20 00	
	do	2156	Turcott, Jean B	20 00	
	Washburn	273	Ryder, Cornelius	20 00	
	Alexandria	1610	Cameron, Duncan	20 00	
	do	3143	McMillan, John	20 00	
	do	3411	Vandrick, Antoine		Services not proved.
	Athol	2142	Larocque, Thomas	20 00	
	Camerontown	1896	Grant, Donald	20 00	
	Curry Hill	1893	Curry, James		Dead.
	Cashions Glen	2685	Grant, Angus	20 00	
	do	1623	McLennan, Hugh	20 00	
	Dalhousie Mills	3487	McDonell, Alexander		Complete for 1st July, 1877.
	Glen Norman	1716	McDougall, Alexander...	20 00	
	do	1895	McDonald, John	20 00	
	do	1831	McMillan, Donald	20 00	
	Greenfield	581	McDonell, Angus	20 00	
	Glenroy	2680	McDonald, Angus	20 00	
	do	1726	McDougald, Ronald	20 00	

PENSIONS TO MILITIAMEN OF 1812-15.—*Continued.*

PROVINCE OF ONTARIO.—*Continued.*

Electoral District.	Post Office.	Number of Case.	Name of Militiaman.	Amount Paid.	Remarks.
				$ cts.	
GLENGARRY.—*Con* Laggan		583	Ferguson, Donald	20 00	
	Laggan	785	McDonell, Angus		Dead.
	do	578	McLellan, Alexander	20 00	
	do	592	McLeod, Alexander	2) 00	
	do	580	McMillan, John	20 00	
	Lancaster	2166	Grant, Alexander		Dead.
	do	3084	McDonald, Alexander	20 00	
	do	1006	McDonald, Ronald	20 00	
	do	3147	McDonald, Hugh	20 00	
	do	1723	McDonell, Alexander	20 00	
	do	2164	McDonell, Allen	20 00	
	do	1900	McDonell, Archibald	20 00	
	do	2695	McDonell, Duncan	20 00	
	do	1720	McDonald, Angus	20 00	
	do	1721	McDougall, John	20 00	
	do	1834	McDougald, Archibald	20 00	
	do	1718	McGillis, Finlay	20 00	
	do	1722	McGillis, Angus	20 00	
	do	1717	McLennan, Robert	20 00	
	do	3406	McDonnell, Alexander		Services not proved.
	Lochiel	579	McIntosh, Angus		Dead.
	do	2889	Marchand, Francis	20 00	
	Martintown	1889	Leclair, Michel	20 00	
	do	1897	McArthur, John		Dead.
	do	2696	Sharron, Gabriel	20 00	
	do	2681	Urquhart, James		Dead.
	do	1713	Grenier, Hyacinthe	20 00	
	do	1899	McDonell, Angus	20 00	
	do	1832	McDonell, Alexander	20 00	
	Notfield	1609	McDonell, Allen	20 00	

PENSIONS TO MILITIAMEN OF 1812-15.—*Continued.*

PROVINCE OF ONTARIO.—*Continued.*

Electoral District.	Post Office.	Number of Case.	Name of Militiaman.	Amount Paid.	Remarks.
				$ cts.	
•GLENGARRY. -*Con*	Notfield	3069	Munro, William	20 00	
	do	2682	Munro David	20 00	
	do	3407	Boyer, Paul		Services not proved.
	do	1005	McDonald, Archibald	20 00	
	do	3297	McDonell, Archibald		Services not proved.
	Rivière Raisin	1892	Dorchester, John	20 00	
	do	1714	Glassford, Little	20 00	
	do	1712	Grant, Richard	20 00	
	do	1711	McDougald, Donald	20 00	
	do	2162	McLennan, Neil	20 00	
	do	1715	McKenzie, Wm.		Dead.
	do	1891	Smith, Duncan	20 00	
	do	1726	Snyder, David		Dead.
	do	1008	McDonald, John	20 00	
	Sandfield	1719	McNeil, John	20 00	
	Summerstown	3146	Rose, John	20 00	
	St. Raphael	1835	McDonald, James	20 00	
	do	1833	McRae, John	20 00	
	Williamstown	1724	Campbell, Donald	20 00	
	do	1728	Ferguson, Alexander		Dead.
	do	2698	Grant, Alexander	20 00	
	do	1727	Flay, John	20 00	
	do	1890	McDonald, Donald	20 00	
	do	2697	McDonald, John	20 00	
	do	1898	McDonell, Wm.	20 00	
	do	2165	McDonell, Alexander		Dead.
	do	2167	McGregor, James	20 00	
	do	2163	Nolan, William		Dead.
	do	1611	Cain, Bernard	20 00	

PENSIONS TO MILITIAMEN OF 1812-15.—*Continued.*

PROVINCE OF ONTARIO.—*Continued.*

Electoral District.	Post Office.	Number of Case.	Name of Militiaman.	Amount Paid.	Remarks.
				$ cts.	
GRENVILLE	Algonquin	1054	Earle, Ephraim	20 00	
	do	2886	Wright, John		No return.
	Bishop's Mills	3158	Bishop, Chancey	20 00	
	Brouseville	514	Curtis, Adam	20 00	
	do	226	Lethernot, Tewsan	20 00	
	Burritt's Rapids	136	Depencier, Luke	20 00	
	Charleyville	1843	Hodge, Timothy	20 00	
	Edwardsburg	184	McIlmoye, James D.	20 00	
	Kemptville	288	Adams, James		No return.
	do	1443	Shaver, Elijah	20 00	
	do	1547	Hemenery, Delver		Services not proved.
	Kilmarnock	1444	Tallman, Charles	20 00	
	Maitland	2329	Jones, Dunham	20 00	
	do	364	McCrae, James	20 00	
	Merrickville	2360	McPearson, Thomas	20 00	
	do	607	Nicholson, Robert	20 00	
	do	451	Rose, Charles	20 00	
	do	1437	Vaughan, John	20 00	
	North Augusta	1051	Landon, William	20 00	
	do	2432	Seely, David	20 00	
	Prescott	3324	Twinning, John	20 00	
	do	2831	Mosher, Henry	20 00	
	do	3161	Marceau, Antoine	20 00	
	do	101	Coons, Jacob	20 00	
	do	1842	Smades, Elijah, B		Dead.
	do	100	Walter, Jacob.	20 00	
	do	1240	Whitney, Comfort		Dead.
	do	2328	Sellick, Ira	20 00	
	Shanley	2660	Forrester, John	20 00	

PENSIONS TO MILITIAMEN OF 1812-15.—*Continued.*

PROVINCE OF ONTARIO.—*Continued.*

Electoral District.	Post Office.	Number of Case.	Name of Militiaman.	Amount Paid.	Remarks.
				$ cts.	
GRENVILLE.—*Con.*	South Gower	460	Pelton, Elijah	20 00	
	do	515	Smith, James	20 00	
	Spencerville	293	Cook, Joseph	20 00	
	do	185	Keeler, George	20 00	
	do	187	King, Stephen		Dead.
	do	177	Lawrence, John		Dead.
GREY	Daywood	3421	Day, Peter		Services not proved.
	Durham	2814	Morden, John C		do
	Meaford	1563	Boucher, Francis H	20 00	
	do	1048	McDonald, John	20 00	
	Owen Sound	1307	McDermid, Hugh	20 00	
	do	159	Belrose, John	20 00	
	do	3042	Hotchkis, Jonthan		Services not proved.
	Shrigley	1317	Wood, Jonah	20 00	
	Thornbury	2048	Burritt, Edmund	20 00	
	Walter's Falls	446	Dyre, Henry	20 00	
HALDIMAND	Canfield	2110	McDonald, William	20 00	
	do	2117	Smith, Lewis	20 00	
	Rainham Centre	2210	Stewart, Benjamin	20 00	
	Selkirk	30	Hare, William	20 00	
	do	32	Ormy, Abraham	20 00	
	Seneca	2219	Smok, John	20 00	
	do	2212	Warner, Young	20 00	
	South Cayuga	3009	Burnham, Oliver	20 00	
	do	2357	Garvey, John	20 00	
	York	534	Nellis, John A	20 00	
	do	723	Sem, Jacob		Dead.
HALTON	Acton	1673	Crips, John	20 00	
	do	2229	Minot, David		Services not proved.

PENSIONS TO MILITIAMEN OF 1812-15.—*Continued.*

PROVINCE OF ONTARIO.—*Continued.*

Electoral District.	Post Office.	Number of Case.	Name of Militiaman.	Amount Paid.	Remarks.
				$ cts.	
HALTON.—*Con*	Acton	1565	Smith, John	20 00	
	Georgetown	1659	Campbell, Alexander	20 00	
	do	628	Grass, Henry	20 00	
	Milton West	2951	Racey, Thomas	20 00	
	Nelson	3014	Bradt, Albert	20 00	
	do	2769	Campbell, Louis	20 00	
	do	1940	Rose, Peter	20 00	
	Oakville	1402	Cleakinson, Warren	20 00	
	do	1837	Mathews, Amos	20 00	
	Palermo	2748	Inglehart, John	20 00	
	Port Nelson	814	Leclair, Peter	20 00	
	Trafalgar	1734	Albertson, William	20 00	
		2228	Freeman, Isaac	20 00	
HAMILTON	Hamilton	1771	Abcowser, Christopher		No return.
	do	15	Bradshaw, George	20 00	
	do	1770	Houle, Jean B.		No return.
	do	2990	Vanevery, Peter		Dead.
	do	2389	David, Thomas	20 00	
	do	3006	Pettit, Elias	20 00	
HASTINGS.	Bannockburn	2194	Roblin, Philip	20 00	
	Belleville	1090	Cariff, Jonas	20 00	
	do	1706	Carscallen, James	20 00	
	do	753	Davis, Robert	20 00	
	do	638	Diamond, Abraham	20 00	
	do	636	Diamond, John	20 00	
	do	44	Diamond, William	20 00	
	do	1705	Empey, Thomas		Dead.
	do	3124	Fralick, Thos. T.	20 00	
	do	810	Height, .	20 00	

PENSIONS TO MILITIAMEN OF 1812-15.—*Continued.*

PROVINCE OF ONTARIO.—*Continued.*

Electoral District.	Post Office.	Number of Case.	Name of Militiaman.	Amount Paid.	Remarks.
				$ cts.	
HASTINGS.—*Con...*	Belleville...............	463	Ketcheson, Elijah.........	20 00	
do	....	6.9	Huyck, Joseph P.	20 00	
do	....	3157	McIntosh, Alexander.....	....	No return.
do	....	461	McTaggart, James........	20 00	
do	....	1380	Ostram, Luke...............	20 00	
do	....	262	Zwick, Philip	20 00	
do	....	2005	Badgley, Cornelius	....	Services not proved.
Blessington..		3149	Hubbel, Peter	....	On list for 1st July, 1877.
Bridgewater.........		2080	Lindsay, Thomas...........	20 00	
do	....	3328	Fortin, Beloni........	20 00	
Cannifton		1371	Jones, Apollo........	....	No return.
do	....	3440	Howard, John	....	Services not proved.
Chapman	....	2979	Parks, James C	20 00	
Foxboro'	....	754	Thrasher, Joseph...........	20 00	
Frankford...........		622	Chisholm, Alexander.....	20 00	
do	....	2709	Smith, John G.	20 00	
do	....	2705	Vanmeer, Zachariah......	20 00	
Harold...............		1626	Cole, William...............	20 00	
do	....	2825	McMillan, Henry...........	20 00	
Halloway	....	3996	Simpson, Patrick....	20 00	
Madoc................		1814	St. Charles, Charles......	20 00	
Marysville............		1874	Young, William.............	20 00	
Philipston		943	Denys, Peter...............	20 00	
do	....	1194	Sills, William...............	20 00	
Queensboro'		2797	Dafoe, Francis...............	20 00	
Spring Brook...		1261	Huff, Isaac	20 00	
Shannonville........		3167	Hill, Joseph...............	20 00	
Stirling		2047	Benedict, Ell...............	20 00	
do	....	1347	Keller, Frederick·.	20 00	

PENSIONS TO MILITIAMEN OF 1812-15.—*Continued.*

PROVINCE OF ONTARIO.—*Continued.*

Electoral District.	Post Office.	Number of Case.	Name of Militiaman.	Amount Paid.	Remarks.	Electoral D
				$ cts.		
HASTINGS.—*Con....*	Stirling	1438	Smith, Amos L............	20 00		KENT........
	do	962	Vancott, David	20 00		
	do	8318	Vandervoort, James......	20 00		
	Trenton	2471	Alger, Charles............	....	No return.	
	do	2298	Davis, Lyman.............	20 00		
	do	1921	Duquette, Etienne........	20 00		
	do	1920	Goulette, François......	....	No return.	
	do	201;	Weaer, Robert............	20 00		
	do	2439	Howaer, John.............	20 00		
	do	2731	Meyers, Tob. Walter	20 00		
	do	2297	Meyers, John W...........	20 00		
	do	2440	Vanderoot, James.......	....	Services not proved.	
	Thomasburg........	2795	Crankight, Jacob	20 00		
	Tweed..............	2981	Rogers, James............	20 00		
	Thurlow............	1876	Grinsolus, Cornelius....	20 00		
	do	462	McMaster, Jacob..........	20 00		
	Walbridge............	461	Ketcheson, Thomas	....	No return.	LAMBTON ..
	do	717	Rose, Samuel E...........	20 00		
HURON..............	Bayfield	1786	Lacourse, Claude	20 00		
	Edmondvi...	81	Picard, Archibald........	....	Services not proved.	
	Gorr.	2358	ook, Jacob...............	....	Services not proved.	
	Walton..............	2546	Perrault, Joseph	20 00		
	Wroxeter..........	308	Kennedy, Samuel.........	20 00		
KINGSTON	Kingston............	338	Leaman, James A.........	2 0		
	do	2341	Penner, Charles	20 00		
	do	1201	Sellars, Robert...........	20 00		
	do	1872	Shibley, David............	20 00		
	do	5	Brown, Christian Julius.	20 00		LANARK ....
	do	2983	Willet, John.............	....	No return.	

PENSIONS TO MILITIAMEN OF 1812-15.—*Continued.*

PROVINCE OF ONTARIO.—*Continued.*

Electoral District.	Post Office.	Number of Case.	Name of Militiaman.	Amount Paid.	Remarks.
				$ cts.	
KENT	Buxton	103	Goulet, Frs. X.	20 00	
	Chatham	2247	Cameron, John	20 00	
	do	1167	Desilets, Joseph	20 00	
	do	1223	Frazter, John	20 00	
	do	1844	Field, Daniel	20 00	
	do	2783	Labute, Pierre	20 00	
	do	3000	Lafrance, Joseph	20 00	
	do	2264	McLeod, Malcolm	20 00	
	do	2999	Thompkins, Nathan	20 00	
	Darrell	543	French, Peter	20 00	
	do	2248	Devens, Abraham		Services not proved.
	Dover, South	542	Charron, Andrew	20 00	
	Dover, East	2996	Lussier, Basile	20 00	
	Harwick	781	Stewart, John	20 00	
	Rondeau	1600	Howey, Stephen	20 00	
	Wallaceburg	2821	Cook, Thomas	20 00	
LAMBTON	Forrest	887	Kilmer, Philip	20 00	
	do	3227	Lounsberry, James	20 00	
	Logieralt	3049	Smith, Henry		Services not proved.
	Moore	1763	Viger, Jean B	20 00	
	do	2717	Robbins, Henry		Services not proved.
	Sarnia	3193	Kiyoshk, Jacob	20 00	
	do	3194	Tacoose	20 00	
	do	3192	Shawaneeee		Dead.
	Waterford	3495	Birtch, Archibald		On list for 1st July, 1877.
	Widder Station	1009	Kennedy, Morris	20 00	
	Wyoming	809	Peterson, David		Dead.
LANARK	Elphin	3269	Hannah, John	20 00	
	Smith's Falls	726	McGillivray, Peter	20 00	

PENSIONS TO MILITIAMEN OF 1812-15.—*Continued.*

PROVINCE OF ONTARIO.—*Continued.*

Electoral District.	Post Office.	Number of Case.	Name of Militiaman.	Amount Paid.	Remarks.
				$ cts.	
LANARK.—*Con*......	Smith's Falls........	406	Shamiour, Francis........	20 00	
	do	227	Ward, Abel R	20 00	
LEEDS................	Caintown	2683	Cain, David Roblins......	20 00	
	do	1620	Miller, Samuel	20 00	
	Chantry...............	2694	Buell, Rinaldo.............	20 00	
	do	2289	Stodard, Arvin........	20 00	
	Delta	2054	Johnson, John..............	20 00	
	do	2260	Wittse, William....	20 00	
	do	2872	Wood, Amos..............	20 00	
	Elgin	1813	Brown, William..........	....	No return.
	do	1806	Halladay, Ebenezer.......	20 00	
	do	1764	Mitchell, Ira	20 00	
	do	1996	Stevens, David	20 00	
	do	2851	Moore, William	20 00	
	Escott	2659	Elliott, Abraham.........	20 00	
	do	1648	Thomas, James	?? 00	
	Farmersville........	1936	Derbyshire, Joseph	20 00	
	do	2359	Parish, Joel	20 00	
	Frankville	733	Humphrey, Henry........	....	Services not proved.
	Gananoque........	1062	Lloyd, John G.............	20 00	
	do	2240	Rosebach, Nicholas......	....	No return.
	Harlem................	191	Chipman, Harry...	20 00	
	Lansdown	2007	Griffin, John..............	20 00	
	Lyndhurst	397	Chase, Benjamin...........	20 00	
	do	2418	Gilfillan, William........	20 00	
	Newborough	1804	Bush, William F	20 00	
	do	2380	Kilborn, John........	20 00	
	Portland	1805	Sheldon, Horace F........	20 00	
	Philipsville..	2397	Brown, Thompson	....	Dead.

PENSIONS TO MILITIAMEN OF 1812-15—Continued.

PROVINCE OF ONTARIO.—Continued.

Electoral District.	Post Office.	Number of Case.	Name of Militiamen.	Amount Paid.	Remarks.
				$ cts.	
LEEDS.—Con	Philipsville	2139	Halloday. Alvin T	20 00	
	Rockport	1984	Edgley, Bo well	20 00	
	do	2679	McCue, Pe er	20 00	
	do	259	Seaman, Smith		Dead.
	do	1983	Wright, William	20 00	
	South Lake	349	Stoliker, John	20 00	
	Sweet's Corner	2053	Sliter, Hiel	20 00	
	Warburton	2232	Sliter, David	20 00	
	Westport	2692	Rorison, Robert D	20 00	
LENNOX	Adolphustown	618	Davis, Henry	20 00	
	do	910	Robbin, Stephen	20 00	
	Bath	1871	Aylworth, Martin		Dead.
	do	935	Bristol, Colman	20 00	
	do	1873	Burlay, William	20 00	
	Ernestown	1398	Amey, Peter	20 00	
	do	570	Link, John	20 00	
	do	2036	Sharp, Lucas	20 00	
	Morven	1014	Smith, Jacob	20 00	
	do	284	Howley, Johnson	20 00	
	do	2750	Johnson, Silas	20 00	
	Mill Haven	2751	Miller, Jacob	20 00	
	Napanee	118	Bezeau, Michel	20 00	
	do	1083	Bristol, John W	20 00	
	do	283	Davy, John	20 00	
	do	678	Deltor, George Hill	20 00	
	do	706	Hawley, John	20 00	
	do	1850	Kennedy, Henry		Left Limits.
	do	1263	Kerby, William	20 00	
	do	351	Kimmerly, Garrett	20 00	

PENSIONS TO MILITIAMEN OF 1812–15.—*Continued.*

PROVINCE OF ONTARIO.—*Continued.*

Electoral District.	Post Office.	Number of Case.	Name of Militiaman.	Amount Paid.	Remarks.
				$ cts.	
LENNOX.—*Con*	Napanee	354	Kimmerly, John	20 00	
	do	1084	Lattimer, William	20 00	
	do	164	Morden, Joseph W	20 00	
	do	550	Oliver, Fr derick	20 00	
	do	738	Schryver, George	20 00	
	do	507	Scott, William	20 00	
	do	119	Shermahorn, Asa	20 00	
	do	353	Shermahorn, Amos	20 00	
	do	2751	Vanalstine, Jonas		Services not proved.
	do	2092	Young, John	20 00	
	do	1152	William, David		Services not proved.
	Odessa	122	Chatterson Joseph	20 00	
	do	220	David, Daniel	20 00	
	do	2195	Lucas, Dennis	20 00	
	do	1221	Parro:t, Jonathan	20 00	
	do	16	Smith, Samuel	20 00	
	do	1166	Vermett, John		Dead.
	do	3428	Leaman, Solomon		On list for 1st July, 1877.
	do	2755	Babcock, Daniel	20 00	
	do	3461	Asselstine, John		Services not proved.
	Parma	737	Dafoe, John	20 00	
	do	16.8	Hulfnail, Jacob	20 00	
	do	1151	Rikely, Jacob	20 00	
	Roblin	352	Pringle, David	20 00	
	do	2792	Young, George		Dead.
	Selby	1159	Dafoe, Daniel	20 00	
	do	117	Benn, Hugh	20 00	
	do	355	Hainer, George	20 00	
	Sillsville	708	Sills, William Bell	20 00	

PENSIONS TO MILITIAMEN OF 1812-15.—*Continued.*

PROVINCE OF ONTARIO.—*Continued.*

Electoral District.	Post Office.	Number of Case.	Name of Militiaman.	Amount Paid.	Remarks.
				$ cts.	
LENNOX.—*Con*	Sillsville	1645	Card, Joseph	20 00	
	Violet	1739	Storms, John		On list for 1st July, 1877.
	Wilton	3057	Babcock, Eli	20 00	
	do	2846	Kellar, Andrew	20 00	
LINCOLN	Beamsville	701	Cook, William	20 00	
	do	921	McKay, William	20 00	
	do	1169	Konkle, Adam	20 00	
	Clinton	1704	Claus, Nicholas	20 00	
	do	1761	House, Patrick	20 00	
	do	2828	Tester, Isaac	20 00	
	Grimsby	2221	Douslough, Jacob	20 00	
	do	1853	Wooberton, Dennis		Services not proved.
	Homer	795	Cudney, Daniel	20 00	
	do	1092	Secord, William Ed	20 00	
	Louth (Township)	1599	McIntee, James	20 00	
	Smithville	2494	Buckbee, Peter	20 00	
	do	2822	Cosby, Eleb	20 00	
	do	2451	Lacey, George	20 00	
	do	2241	Merritt, David		Dead.
	do	2811	Merritt, Robert	20 00	
	do	3050	Nelson, Daniel		Dead.
	do	2706	White, Eli		Dead.
	St. Catherines	1196	Bessey, John	20 00	
	do	2720	Hartwell, Joseph	20 00	
	do	1184	Haines, Adam	20 00	
	do	530	Hill, Solomon	20 00	
	do	2387	Jones, William		Dead.
	do	2351	Ousterhant, Henry		Dead.
	do	1049	Tinlin, James	20 00	

PENSIONS TO MILITIAMEN OF 1812-15.—*Continued.*

PROVINCE OF ONTARIO.—*Continued.*

Electoral District.	Post Office.	Number of Case.	Name of Militiaman.	Amount Paid.	Remarks.
				$ cts.	
LONDON	London	2820	Stickel, Peter	20 00	
	do	1962	Corsant, Christopher	20 00	
	do	272	Draker, Phineas	20 00	
	do	1360	Glassford, William	20 00	
	do	2500	Lewis, Levi	20 00	
	do	1098	McMartin, William	20 00	
	do	1657	Pixley, Robert	20 00	
	do	3333	McDonald, Donald		Services not proved.
	do	3455	Reynolds, James		Services not proved.
MIDDLESEX	Belmont	3020	Dinnor, Joseph	20 00	
	Byron	1932	Cornell, Aaron	20 00	
	Caradoc	621	Cornwell, Robert	20 00	
	Crumlin	1178	Young, John K.	26 00	
	Delaware	3175	Chief, Tom	20 00	
	do	3121	Cudney, Ferris	20 00	
	do	3197	Tomego, John	20 00	
	Glen Willow	2727	Moor, William	20 00	
	Lambeth	1361	Fortner, Andrew		No return.
	do	1050	Cornwall, Jesse	20 00	
	Longwood	3176	Dolsen, Isaac		No return.
	do	1601	Grote, Simon	20 00	
	do	3177	King, George	20 00	
	do	3178	Snake, Thomas	20 00	
	Mosa	2498	Badine, Nicholas	20 00	
	Mount Brydges	1122	Flanagan, Barnabas	20 60	
	do	410	Meyers, Benjamin	20 00	
	do	1183	Heron, Andrew	20 00	
	do	77	Reynolds, David	20 00	
	do	942	Weishuhn, James		Dead.

PENSIONS TO MILITIAMEN OF 1812-15.—*Continued.*

PROVINCE OF ONTARIO.—*Continued.*

Electoral District.	Residence.	Number of Case.	Name of Militiaman.	Amount Paid.	Remarks.
				$ cts.	
MIDDLESEX.—*Con.*	Mount Brydges	1523	Depatis, John		Services not proved.
	Napier	3024	Emrick, Francis	20 00	
	Newbury	1180	Henry, George	20 00	
	Parkhill	1450	Fike, Daniel	20 00	
	do	79	Emery, John		Services not proved.
	Sylvan	2350	Brown, George	20 00	
	Tempo	1524	Bennett, Jesse	20 00	
	do	2222	Campbell, Isaac	20 00	
	Thorndale	2762	Jackson, Henry	20 00	
	Westminster	343	Griffith, Ezra	20 00	
MONCK	Cainboro'	3275	Daughnue, Joseph	20 00	
	Dunville	2211	Monte, Adam	20 00	
	do	2715	Vaughan, Daniel	20 00	
	Fenwick	1848	Lambert, John	20 00	
	do	2124	Pattison, John	20 00	
	North Pelham	2463	Disher, David	20 00	
	do	2464	Disher, William	20 00	
	do	2462	Metler, David	20 00	
	do	2466	Comfort, John	20 00	
	Pelbam Union	844	Moore, David	20 00	
	do	845	Moore, John	20 00	
	Ridgville	2370	Merritt, John	20 00	
	Rosedene	1687	Furlow, Koonrad	20 00	
	do	1320	Lane, Joseph	20 00	
	St. Anns	2495	Mingle, John	20 00	
	do	3458	Frease, Peter		On list for 1st July, 1877.
	Stromness	1700	Benner, George	20 00	
	do	2468	Furry, William	20 00	
	Welland Port	2429	McPherson, John	20 00	

PENSIONS TO MILITIAMEN OF 1812-15.—*Continued.*

PROVINCE OF ONTARIO.—*Continued.*

Electoral District.	Post Office.	Number of Case.	Name of Militiaman.	Amount Paid.	Remarks.
				$ cts.	
MONCK.—*Con.*	Welland Port........	2430	Vaughan, Jacob.............	20 00	
	do	2291	Robins, John..............	20 00	
MUSKOKA.............	Baysville............	3096	Anderson, John............	20 00	
	Raymond.............	38	Onderkirk, Henry........	20 00	
NIAGARA	Niagara	843	McFarland, Duncan......	20 00	
	Virgil..................	842	Thompson, Jas. Smith...	20 00	
	do	2206	Lawrence, George B.....	20 00	
NORFOLK	Bloomsburg..	1410	Barber, Moses......	20 00	
	do	1407	Kitchen, William..........	20 00	
	do	1411	Mumo, George.............	20 00	
	Boston......	1836	Nelles, Abraham..........	20 00	
	Charlotteville	1426	Jackson, John..............	....	Dead.
	do	1854	Earle, Lewis......	20 00	
	Clear Creek	528	McEwan, William.........	20 00	
	Courtland	3373	Johnson, Peter.............	20 00	
	Delhi	2215	Kemp, Abraham	20 00	
	do	2157	Shaver, John..............	20 00	
	do	1961	Sovereene, Henry	20 00	
	Forrestville..........	2702	Kern, Christopher	20 00	
	Guysboro	2875	Kitchen, Henry	....	No return.
	do	1161	Mabee, Pinkney............	20 00	Dead.
	Hartford.............	2707	Wilcox, John	20 00	
	Houghton Centre..	1422	Buckner, Philip............	20 00	
	Kelvin................	2300	Huffman, Henry......	20 00	
	Lynedoch	1183	Dell, Joseph	20 00	
	do	1373	Disbrow, Ira	20 00	
	do	825	Wilson, Peter..............	20 00	
	do	1182	Mathews, John.......	20 00	
	Lynville..............	2101	Cudney, James.......	20 00	

PENSIONS TO MILITIAMEN OF 1812-15.—*Continued.*

PROVINCE OF ONTARIO.—*Continued.*

Electoral District.	Post Office.	Number of case.	Name of Militiaman.	Amount Paid.	Remarks.
				$ cts.	
NORFOLK.—*Con*	Normandale	1585	Ferris, James	20 00	
	do	1312	Wood, Thomas	20 00	
	Pleasant Hill	1733	Auger, Charles	20 00	
	do	2434	Chambers, Joseph	20 00	
	Port Dover	3419	Courtland, Old		Services not proved.
	Port Royal	1432	Foster, Edward	20 00	
	do	1434	Beaumivart, Henry		Services not proved.
	Port Rowen	1431	Saxton, Jno. H	20 00	
	do	1433	Shoemaker, Peter	20 00	
	do	1435	Williams, Titus	20 00	
	do	2740	Dickson, Daniel		On list for 1st July, 1877.
	Port Ryerse	1408	Buckner, Thelor	20 00	
	do	2701	Ryerse, George	20 00	
	do	1193	Wood, David	20 00	
	do	2100	Winters, Emmanuel		Services not proved.
	Round Plaines	1666	McDonald, John	20 00	
	do	1420	Sovereen, Laurence	20 00	
	do	3445	Mossear, John		Services not proved.
	Simcoe	1421	Austin, Philip	20 00	
	do	1419	Culver, Adam	20 00	
	do	1416	Disbrow, Almond	20 00	
	do	730	Hendershot, Daniel	20 00	
	do	2103	Karr, John		No return.
	do	1425	Mills, John	20 00	
	do	1415	Stockwell, Isaac	20 00	
	do	2102	Walker, James	20 00	
	do	1409	Wycoff, Peter	20 00	
	do	1185	Youngs, Abraham	20 00	
	do	1651	Walsh, F. Legh		Declined to receive allowance

PENSIONS TO MILITIAMEN OF 1812-15.—*Continued.*

PROVINCE OF ONTARIO.—*Continued.*

Electoral District.	Post Office.	Number of Case.	Name of Militiaman.	Amount Paid.	Remarks.
				$ cts.	
NORFOLK.—*Con.*	St. Williams	1331	McCall, Daniel	20 00	
	do	1340	Glover, Charles	20 00	
	Townsend Centre	1413	Lewis, James Sam	20 00	
	do	1780	Haviland, Benjamin	20 00	
	Victoria	2055	Munro, Robert	20 00	
	Waterford	1412	Bowly, Adam	20 00	
	do	1414	Merrill, Charles	20 00	
	do	1586	Scovell, Samuel		Dead.
	do	1417	Slaght, William	20 00	
	Windham	1423	Dell, Richard	20 00	
	do	1372	Shaver, Isaac	20 00	
NORTHUMBER-LAND	Baltimore	3467	Parker, Reuben W		Services not proved.
	Bomanton	2386	Brisbin, William	20 00	
	do	2267	Purdy, Benjamin	20 00	
	Brighton	2785	Colby, Timothy	20 00	
	do	3071	Cryderman, Joseph		Left limits.
	do	1558	Gibson, Joseph	20 00	
	do	1560	Lawson, John M	20 00	
	do	1561	Shear, David		No return.
	do	1559	Sprung, John	20 00	
	do	837	Thompkins, Caleb	20 00	
	do	1946	Vansicklin, Ferdinand	20 00	
	Castleton	65	Blakely, Samuel		Dead.
	do	445	Gaffield, Jonathan	20 00	
	do	290	Moore, James	20 00	
	do	64	Phillips, James	20 00	
	do	63	Williams, Benjamin	20 00	
	Cobourg	2716	Culver, Abraham	20 00	
	do	2480	Kelly, N. F. H.	20 00	

PROVINCE OF ONTARIO.—Continued.

Electoral District.	Residence.	Number of Case.	Name of Militiaman.	Amount Paid.	Remarks.
				$ cts.	
NORTHUMBERL'D.	Cobourg	344	McCarthy, John	20 00	
	do	831	Perry, Ebenezer		Dead.
	Codrington	1944	Orser, David	20 00	
	Colborne	1244	Huycke, John P	20 00	
	Dartford	1068	Young, Joseph	20 00	
	do	2225	Darling, John		Services not proved.
	Eddystone	1943	Eddy Harden	20 00	
	do	2151	Purdy, James	20 00	
	do	3239	Tucker, Isaac	20 00	
	Gore's Landing	2777	Harris, Joseph	20 00	
	Grafton	2149	Hinman, Turnam	20 00	
	Haldimand	2150	Sweet, Jared Lewis		Dead.
	Hamilton, Township.)	993	Ash, Hiram	20 00	
	Munich	2257	Sundy, John		Dead.
	Murray	1971	Preston, Benjamin	20 00	
	Norham	2174	Cornelius, Nicholas	20 00	
	do	1367	Reynolds, Benjamin	20 00	
	do	1366	Weller, Elakam	20 00	
	Rosa	1919	Maybee, Abraham	20 00	
	Smithfield	1948	Johnson, Henry H		Dead.
	Vernonville	2388	Purdy, James	20 00	
	do	3076	Norton, James		Services not proved.
	Warworth	2716	Dubuc, François	20 00	
	do	1365	Hicks, Benjamin	20 00	
	do	963	Sexton, George		Dead.
	Wicklow	1177	Hubbel, Martin	20 0	
	do	3224	Doolittle, Ephriam	20 00	
OXFORD.	Beachville	1142	Fuller, Ira	20 00	
	do	1186	Moote, Richard	20 00	

PROVINCE OF ONTARIO.—*Continued.*

Electoral District.	Residence.	Number of Case.	Name of Militiaman.	Amount Paid.	Remarks.
				$ cts.	
OXFORD.—(*Con.*)...	Burgessville.........	3019	Cameron, Finlay..........	20 00	
	Drimbo...............	1119	Markile, Abraham	....	Services not proved.
	Ingersoll.........	2452	Allen, Weston.............	20 00	
	do	2477	Brown, Brinton Paine...	20 00	
	do	2929	Hurtch, Levi.............	20 00	
	do	2109	Hopkins Caleb	20 00	
	do	2205	Rice, David	20 00	
	do	2478	Comfort, Sage.............	20 00	
	Norwich.............	1035	Collard, Robert...........	20 00	
	do	2745	Woodrow, J. Gill...	20 00	
	Otterville..........	1188	Horning, Aaron..........	20 00	
	do	1969	Piper, Thomas	....	Dead.
	do	1242	Taylor, Richard	20 00	
	Oxford Station......	1597	Woodraw, Edmond.......	20 00	
	do	1869	Smith, Daniel.............	20 00	
	Princetown..........	3277	Lounsberry, James	....	Services not proved.
	Tilsonburg	1769	Vannorman, Abraham...	20 00	
	Woodstock..........	1785	Clement, Samuel T......	20 00	
	do	2106	Tree, John B.............	20 00	
ONTARIO.............	Brougham..........	3264	Arnold, Isaac.............	....	On list for 1st July, 1877.
	Cannington.........	2254	Laviolette, Pierre	20 00	
	Columbus....	2112	Bedford, David	20 00	
	Dunbarton..........	516	Stoner, Abraham..	20 00	
	Dufferin's Creek....	3264	Arnold, Isaac	....	On list for 1st July, 1877.
	Oshawa.............	2111	Fisher, Henry.............	20 00	
	do	2220	Henry, Thomas.......... ...	20 00	
	do	1841	Martin, Moses.............	20 00	
	do	3161	Adams, John.............	....	Services not proved.
	Port Perry...		Haight, Harrison..........	20 00	

PENSIONS TO MILITIAMEN OF 1812-15.—*Continued.*

PROVINCE OF ONTARIO.—*Continued.*

Electoral District.	Post Office	Number of Case.	Name of Militiaman.	Amount Paid.	Remarks.
				$ cts.	
ONTARIO.—*Con.*	Prince Albert	1406	Ta; '~r, Robert	20 00	
do	do	3292	Badgely, Rozelle	20 00	
	Rama	3337	Simcoe, John	20 00	
	Rathburn	3255	Dafoe, William R.	20 00	
	Whitby	558	Cochrane, Samuel	20 00	
	do	2470	Palmer, John	20 00	
	do	587	Perry, Daniel	20 00	
PEEL	Brampton	1701	Ostrander, James.	20 00	
	do	718	Shook, Jacob	20 00	
	Campbell's Cross	1504	Brooks, Cooper	20 00	
	Cooksville	1811	Silverthorne, Joseph	20 00	
	do	1401	Wilcox, Amos	20 00	
	Credit	2908	Malloy, John		No return.
PETERBOROUGH	Blairton	3048	Dafoe, Conrad	20 00	
	do	2756	Embury, Valentine	20 00	
	Hastings	1571	Huff, Charles	20 00	
	do	3434	Garrat, Thomas		Services not proved.
	Norwood	2158	Cope, Jacob		Dead.
PERTH	Fullarton	535	Davis, William	20 00	
PRESCOTT	Caledonia	3408	Calp, Moses		On list for 1st July, 1877.
	Curran	3065	Burton, James	20 00	
	do	2972	Presly, George	20 00	
	do	2885	Bissonnette, Jean M.	20 00	
	do	3313	Chatelin, Etienne	20 00	
	do	3376	Desrochers, Jean B.		Services not proved.
	L'Orignal	3135	Charlebois, Hyacinthe		Dead.
	Plantagenet	2428	Plouff, Pierre	20 00	
	do	3417	McGregor, Duncan		Services not proved.
	St. Eugene	2191	La Rocque, Francis	20 00	

PENSIONS TO MILITIAMEN OF 1812-15.—*Continued.*

PROVINCE OF ONTARIO.—*Continued.*

Electoral District.	Post Office.	Number of Case.	Name of Militiaman.	Amount Paid.	Remarks.
				$ cts.	
PRESCOTT.—*Con*...	St. Eugene............	2611	Pool, Timothy............	20 00	
	do	2440	Sova, Jean B	20 00	
	do	2337	Beaudry, Louis............	20 00	
	do	2400	Daoust, Joseph	20 00	
	do	1906	Deschamps, François....	20 00	
	do	1914	Menard, Hyacinthe........	20 00	
	do	2325	McKay, André	....	Dead.
	do	1905	Routhier, Charles.........	20 00	
	do	2612	Titly, Réné Charles	20 00	
	do	3265	Seguin, Michel............	20 00	
	Vankleek Hill......	2670	Carrier, Louis.............	20 00	
	do	2613	Seguin, Joseph............	20 00	
PRINCE EDWARD.	Albury	1534	Dempsey, Peter	....	Dead.
	do	1970	Dempsey, Isaac	....	Dead.
	Amelinsburg	1430	Huycks, Cornelius...	....	Dead.
	do	2708	Lambert, John.............	20 00	
	do	1945	Tillotson, John	20 00	
	Bloomfield............	1016	Cannon, Abraham........	20 00	
	do	1017	Cooper, James....	20 00	
	do	2180	Leavens, Daniel..........	20 00	
	do	2183	Leavens, Eliphalet........	20 00	
	Cherry Valley	862	Burlingham, Parnum.....	....	Dead
	do	868	Spencer, James Potter...	20 00	
	Consecon	1298	Squier, Gibbs	20 00	
	do	1399	Young, John...............	20 00	
	do	1069	Pierson, James.....	20 00	
	Demorestville	1170	Roblin, Jacob............	....	Dead.
	do	1176	Parks, Nathaniel............	20 00	
	do	2826	Keltner, Simeon............	20 00	

PENSIONS TO MILITIAMEN OF 1812-15.—*Continued.*

PROVINCE OF ONTARIO.—*Continued.*

Electoral District.	Post Office.	Number of Case.	Name of Militiaman.	Amount Paid.	Remarks.
				$ cts.	
PRINCE EDWARD.	Green Point	870	Roblin, Lévis	20 00	
	do	1174	Short, Jacob	20 00	
	Hallowell	864	Fry, Abraham	20 00	
	do	803	Yerex, William	20 00	
	Hillier	1245	Smith, Lyman	20 00	
	do	1128	Rutter, Alexander		Services not proved.
	Milford	1953	Hughes, Jacob	20 00	
	North Port	1173	Mori n, Joseph	20 00	
	Picton	1018	Bristol, Benjamin	20 00	
	do	1400	David, Thomas.	20 00	
	do	87i	Gerou, John		Dead.
	do	865	Hover, Jacob	20 00	
	do	2788	Johnson, Joseph	20 00	
	do	860	Lazier, Abraham	20 00	
	do	909	Martin, Jonathan		Dead.
	do	2188	Orser, Elijah	20 00	
	do	402	Peterson, Jacob	20 00	
	do	1175	Richards, John	20 00	
	do	2040	Wood, T. Smith	20 00	
	Prinyer	950	Bongard, Conrad	20 00	
	Point Traverse	1462	McCrimmon, Duncan	20 00	
	Rednersville	1847	Rush, James Cobus	20 00	
	do	2367	Snider, John	20 00	
	Ross More	2739	McWilliams, James	20 00	
	West Lake	2185	Mastin, John	20 00	
	Wellington	3451	Garrat, William		On list for 1st July, 1877.
RUSSELL	Billings' Bridge	179	Pillar, John.	20 00	
	do	1569	Shelp, Christopher	20 00	
	do	2676	Hawn, Peter	20 00	

PENSIONS TO MILITIAMEN OF 1812-15—*Continued.*

PROVINCE OF ONTARIO.—*Continued.*

Electoral District.	Post Office.	Number of Case.	Name of Militiamen.	Amount Paid.	Remarks.
				$ cts.	
RUSSELL.—*Con*	Billings' Bridge. ...	1703	Munro, Will am............	20 00	
	do	265	Smythe, William.........	20 00	
	do	2348	Goodman, Peter..........	20 00	
	do	2159	Sabourin, François.........		Dead.
	do	1701	McArthur, Donald		Dead.
	Clarence Creek.....	1468	Chalifoux, Jean B	20 00	
	do	3012	Robillard, Jean B	20 00	
	do	3371	Belanger, Jean B...........		Services not proved.
	Embrun;...............	648	Lalande, Charles	20 00	
	do	3087	Burel, Jean B......		Services not proved.
	Orleans	3118	Defort, Jean B..............	20 00	
	Osgoode...............	2658	Belanger, François	20 00	
	Ramsay's Corner...	2684	McMillan, Alpin	20 00	
SIMCOE..	Barrie	2723	Simpson, James...........		No return.
	do	846	Montgomery, John........	20 00	
	Churchill.............	3201	Wilson, Hiram R...........	20 00	
	Collingwood.........	2365	Hollinshead, Jacob.	20 00	
	do	2224	McDonnell, John.		Dead.
	do	3126	Neff, Clement	20 00	
	Maple Valley........	2807	Lower, Henry.............	20 00	
	Milburst...............	2239	Williams, George ....,	20 00	
	New Lowell	60	Switzer, Daniel	20 00	
	Orillia	3486	Gaudour, Antoine........		Services not proved.
	Penetanguishene...	620	Brissette, Hypolyte..	20 00	
	do ...	802	Cadieux, André	20 00	
	do ...	1505	Desaulniers, Louis		Dead.
	do ...	576	Moreau, Joseph......	20 00	
	Thornton.............	2277	Vanevery, William..	20 00	
STORMONT.............	Aultsville	1022	Cramer, Francis..	2u 00	

PENSIONS TO MILITIAMEN OF 1812-15. *Continued.*

PROVINCE OF ONTARIO.—*Continued.*

Electoral District.	Post Office.	Number of Case.	Name of Militiaman.	Amount Paid.	Remarks.
				$ cts.	
STORMONT.—*Con* ..	Aultaville	2664	Ault, John......................	20 00	
	do	2673	Gallinger, George M	20 00	
	do	2690	Gallinger, George..........	20 00	
	do	2677	Haines, John C..............	20 00	
	do	2602	Ross, Michael..............	20 00	
	do	2874	Vandette, Simon	....	Dead.
	do	2661	Wagner, Solomon	20 00	
	do	1024	Hickeley, John.............	20 00	
	Farren's Point......	2675	Campbell, James..........	20 00	
	do	2669	Dafoe, John	20 00	
	Lunenburg...........	2674	Prosser, Jesse	20 00	
	do	2665	Shaver, Jacob..............	20 00	
	Monckland	2655	McIntosh, William	20 00	
	Moulinette............	1270	Annable, George..........	20 00	
	do	1010	Brownell, Stephen......	....	Dead.
	do	2668	Moss, Thomas	20 00	
	do	2878	Waldroff, John.......	20 00	
	do	1266	Wood, William.....	20 00	
	Newington	2691	Dixon, Robert F............	20 00	
	do	2663	Eligh, David......	20 00	
	do	2688	Snetsinger, Frederick ...	20 00	
	do	2687	Wiserman, William.... ..	20 00	
	do	2686	Hoople, Michael...	....	Services not proved.
	Osnabruck	3342	Stillwill, John	20 00	
	do	2666	Warner, Adam C..........	20 00	
	do	2667	Weart, George C..........	20 00	
	South Finch.........	2672	Steenburg, Peter..........	20 00	
TORONTO..............	Toronto	2910	Ryerson, George..........	20 00	
	do	1496	Bright, John..............	20 00	

PENSIONS TO MILITIAMEN OF 1812-15.—*Continued.*

PROVINCE OF ONTARIO.—*Continued.*

Electoral District.	Post Office.	Number of Case.	Name of Militiaman.	Amount Paid.	Remarks.
				$ cts.	
TORONTO.—*Con*....	Toronto	2904	Wright, E. G. S............	....	No return.
	do	533	White, Isaac...............	20 00	
	do	3165	Kabdobgecgwen, Peter.	....	Services not proved.
	do	3168	Moses, Tace...............	....	Services not proved.
	do	3164	Nawash, James...........	....	Services not proved.
	do	3166	Sunday, Chief John......	....	Services not proved.
VICTORIA............	Dalrymple............	2094	Chrysler, John G.........	20 00	
	Little Britain	1059	Yerex, Isaac...............	20 00	
	Victoria Station ...	2728	Glover, Francis...........	....	Dead.
WATERLOO............	Conestogo............	670	Freeman, John	20 00	
	Galt.	2113	McAffe, Daniel...........	20 00	
	do	1900	Shupe, James.............	....	Left limits.
	do	2396	Cunning, James..........	20 00	
	Preston...............	3021	Snyder, Adam L..........	20 00	
WELLAND	Allanburg............	2718	Allison, Thomas..........	20 00	
	Clifton...............	2719	Young, Philip	....	No return.
	Drummondville.....	2861	Cook, Noah...............	20 00	
	Humber:one	2268	Clendenning, Robert....	20 00	
	do	1950	Doan, Levis	20 00	
	do	1910	Kinnard, Sela.......	20 00	
	do	1953	Steele, David.............	20 00	
	Port Colborne	513	Davis, Samuel......... ...	....	Services not proved.
	Port Robinson.....	2802	Heaslip, Samuel..........	20 00	
	Ridgeway	1815	Bearss, Joseph...........	20 00	
	do	325	Palmer, Lewis	20 00	
	Stamford............	29-9	Thompson, Benjamin....	20 00	
	do	2798	Hyatt, James	20 00	
	Stevensville	778	Huffman, George.........	20 00	
	Thorold	2808	Lampman, Mathias......	20 00	

PENSIONS TO MILITIAMEN OF 1812–15.—*Continued.*

PROVINCE OF ONTARIO.—*Continued.*

Electoral District.	Post Office.	Number of Case.	ame of Militiaman.	Amount Paid.	Remarks.
				$ cts.	
WELLAND.—*Con* ...	Thorold	920	Kelly, Isaac.	20 00	
	do	1319	Yocom, Peter	20 00	
	Welland	2133	Cummer, Daniel.	20 00	
	do	1849	Yocom, Jesse	20 00	
WELLINGTON	Eden Mills	839	Ball, Peter Maine	20 00	
	Garafraxa	2014	Loree, James	20 00	
	Guelph	1564	Staves, Joshua	20 00	
	Harriston.	3159	Wright, Malcolm	20 00	
	Ospring	3160	Wedge, John		Services not proved.
	Rockwood	1672	Soper, Samuel.	20 00	
	Rothsay	42	Calkins, Elijah S	20 00	
WENTWORTH	Alberton	210	Trowbridge. John	20 00	
	Aldershot	2364	Fonger, David..	20 00	
	do	2365	Fonger, George	20 00	
	Ancaster	1909	Aikman, John.	20 00	
	do	2787	Downs, Timothy		No return.
	do	2772	Snider, Frederick	20 00	
	do	2395	Wilson, Samuel	20 00	
	do	2127	Rymal, Joseph	20 00	
	Binbrook	2123	Flock, John	20 00	
	Dundas	3228	Mainville, Mark	20 00	
	do	1191	McDavid, James		Services not proved.
	Elfrida	2737	Sweazy, Andrew	20 00	
	Jerseyville	2704	Vansickle, William	20 00	
	Lynden	2528	Kaler, John	20 00	
	do	3005	Keley, Peter B	20 00	
	Mill Grove	2774	Bradt, David	20 00	
	do	2770	Thompson, William	20 00	
	Mount Albion	2298	Fellker, Frederick	20 00	

PENSIONS TO MILITIAMEN OF 1812-15.--Continued.

PROVINCE OF ONTARIO.—Continued.

Electoral District.	Post Office.	Number of Case.	Name of Militiaman.	Amount Paid.	Remarks.
				$ cts.	
WENTWORTH-Con	North Glanford	2779	Hagle, Jacob.	....	Dead.
	Stoney Creek........	1276	Combs, James.............	20 00	
	do	2330	Carpenter, Charles.......	20 00	
	do	1275	Green, William............	20 00	
	do	2290	Utter, Henry.	20 00	
	Troy	3004	Misener, Peter.............	20 00	
	Waterdown..........	2773	King, William	....	Dead.
	do	2771	Snider, Philip.............	....	Dead.
	Winona	1179	Smith, Silas	20 00	
	West Flamboro'....	1781	Ramsay, John.............	20 00	
YORK............	Box Grove............	3073	Moore, Peter.............	20 00	
	Bloomington........	3399	Fenton, William	....	On list for 1st July, 1877.
	do	2736	Johnson, Vincent..........	....	Dead.
	do	1935	Perkins, John.............	20 00	
	Buttonville...........	1345	Button, Francis,...........	20 00	
	do	1064	Stiver, John H.............	20 00	
	Danforth	1332	Heron, John	20 00	
	do	2217	Palmer, James.............	20 00	
	do	2737	Elson, Henry.............	....	On list for 1st July, 1877.
	Edgley.......	2461	Kaiser, Jacob	20 00	
	Eglington	88	Snider, Martin.............	20 00	
	Eversley.............	671	Wells, John.............	20 00	
	Ellesmere............	2732	Thompson, Archibald....	20 00	
	do	2742	Thompson, Richard.......	20 00	
	Holland Landing...	171	Wilson, R. Titus........	20 00	
	Keswick.............	2278	Crittendam, Amos........	20 00	
	do	2349	Draper, Luther............	20 00	
	Kettleby........	2744	Boudwin, Alexander......	20 00	
	Lansing	2794	Miller, James.......	20 00	

PENSIONS TO MILITIAMEN OF 1812-15.—*Continued.*

PROVINCE OF ONTARIO.—*Continued.*

Electoral District.	Post Office	Number of Case.	Name of Militiaman.	Amount Paid.	Remarks.
				$ cts.	
YORK.—*Con*	Lansing	1364	Miller, Jacob	20 00	
	Leskay	2198	Ross, Robert	20 00	
	do	2791	Wells, Job	20 00	
	Lemonville	2216	Pipher, William	20 00	
	Ma' .om	1663	Crosby, James	20 00	
		2721	Herrick, Lyman		No return.
	do	3079	Shell, Henry C		No return.
		2767	Quanty, Frederick	20 00	
	Mongolia	2713	Boyle, John	20 00	
	Newmarket	163	Mosier, Thomas		Dead.
	do	728	Roe, William	20 00	
	Nobleton	2815	Coddy, Aaron	20 00	
	Pine Orchard	2810	Hayes' John	20 00	
	Queensville	826	Graham, Richard	20 00	
	Ringwood	2114	Smith, Francis	20 00	
	Roach's Point	198	Payson, Ephriam R	20 00	
	Scarboro'	2034	Hough, Joseph	20 00	
	do	1333	Jones, James	20 00	
	do	1239	Stoner, Peter	20 00	
	Stouffville	1934	Kester, Philip	20 00	
	Unionville	841	Stiver Francis	20 00	
	Vachell	2044	Hartt, Joseph	20 00	
	do	2043	Mitchell, Darius	20 00	
	do	2042	Morton, Samuel	20 00	
	Whitchurch, Township.	84	Vannostrand, Cornelius.	20 00	

PENSIONS TO MILITIAMEN OF 1812-15.—*Continued.*

PROVINCE OF QUEBEC.

Electoral District.	Post Office.	Number of Case.	Name of Militiaman.	Amount Paid.	Remarks.
				$ cts.	
ARGENTEUIL	Lachute	1839	Haines, William		Dead.
	St. Andrews	2608	Charlebois, Joseph	20 00	
	do	2603	Burwash, Mathew	20 00	
	do	2435	Guilbault, Gabriel	20 00	
	do	2436	Hyde, George		Dead.
	do	2437	Larocque, Pierre	20 00	
	do	2927	Pilon, Alexandre	20 00	
	do	2612	Renaud, Louis	20 00	
ARTHABASKA	Arthabaskaville	2580	Beauchêne, Charles	20 00	
	do	2577	Demers, Augustin	20 00	
	do	2575	Ouellet, Louis		Dead.
	Chester	2574	Oamiré, Charles	20 00	
	do	1627	Gosselin, Joachim	20 00	
	do	2576	Paquet, Jean B	20 00	
	do	2641	Roux, Prudent	20 00	
	Stanfold	2549	Bourré, Joseph	20 00	
	do	2613	Marchand, Pierre	20 00	
	do	3082	Leblanc, Franc		Services not proved.
	St. Valere	1882	Bibeau, Francois	20 00	
	Tynwick	162	Raiche, Amable	20 00	
BEAUHARNOIS	Beauharnois	2019	Charlebois, Jean B	20 00	
	do	2017	Hebert, Louis	20 00	
	do	1858	Lebœuf, Paul	20 00	
	do	2018	Tondu, Joseph	20 00	
	St. Clement	3122	Laberge, Guillaume		Services not proved.
	St. Etienne	650	Tessier, Jacques	20 00	
	do	1522	Montpetit	20 00	
	St. Louis de Gonzague	2138	Lamarre, Joseph	20 00	
	do	651	Grenier, Pierre		Dead.

PENSIONS TO MILITIAMEN OF 1812-15.—*Continued.*

PROVINCE OF QUEBEC.—*Continued.*

Electoral District.	Post Office.	Number of Case.	Name of Militiaman.	Amount Paid.	Remarks.
				$ cts.	
BEAUHARNOIS......	St. Louis de Gonzague	1335	Guimond, Joseph..........	20 00	
	do ...	640	Prejent, Jean B	20 00	
	do ...	1606	Prejent, Joseph	20 00	
	do ...	3133	Lafebvre, Joachim	20 00	
	St. Stanislas.........	1378	Bertrand, Francois........	20 00	
	do	3139	Lepage, Louis	20 00	
	do	1328	Mabeu, Bartbelemi........	20 00	
	St. Timothée	2074	Bombardier, Michel........	20 00	
	do	2073	Faubert, François........	20 00	
	do	2072	Leduc, Charles............	20 00	
	do	2080	Legault, François	20 00	
	do	2535	Poirier, Joachim	20 00	
	do	2078	Poirier, Hyacinthe	20 00	
	do	2077	Scott, André............	20 00	
	do	2075	Vallée, Jean B............	20 00	
	Valleyfield...........	2313	Cardinal, Joseph..........	20 00	
	do	2317	Corbeille, Pierre	20 00	
	do	2314	French, Ambr	20 00	
	do	2311	Galarneau, Loui B	20 00	
	do	2316	Quenneville, François...	20 00	
	do	2315	Tessier, Lambert..........	20 00	
	do	2310	Vernier, Joseph..........	20 00	
	do	2081	Viau, Alexis..............	20 00	
	do	2312	Hebert, Jacques..........	20 00	
	do	3414	Lefebvre, Joseph..........	....	Services not proved.
BAGOT..........	Acton Vale..........	43	Denommé, Frs. X.	20 00	
	do	3259	Duperon, Frs	20 00	
	Springton	3459	Perreault, François.......	....	Services not proved.

PENSIONS TO MILITIAMEN OF 1812-15.—*Continued.*

PROVINCE OF QUEBEC.—*Continued.*

Electoral District.	Post Office.	Number of Case.	Name of Militiaman.	Amount Paid.	Remarks.
				$ cts.	
BAGOT.—*Con*	St. Dominique	2602	Despart, Jean F		Dead.
	do	776	Dion, Francois		Services not proved.
	St. Ephrem	2601	Dion, Jean B	20 00	
	St Hélène	2140	Desantals, Pierre	20 00	
	do	216	Galarneau, Joseph	20 00	
	do	666	Michaud, Joseph	20 00	
	do	806	Vaillant, Alexis	20 00	
	do	1109	Froment, F. X		Services not proved.
	St. Hughes	989	Blanchet, Jacques	20 00	
	do	981	Chagnon-Larose, J. B...	20 00	
	do	969	Letœuf, Louis	20 00	
	do	991	Petit, Frs. X	20 00	
	do	988	Richard, Basile	20 00	
	do	992	Tremblay, Joseph	20 00	
	do	3249	Rousseau, François	20 00	
	do	3248	Berard, Joseph	20 00	
	St. Liboire	923	Charbonneau, André	20 00	
	St. Pie	6	Amelotte, Joseph	20 00	
	do	2272	Bonnier, Jacques	20 00	
	do	612	Chartier Philippe		Dead.
	do	614	Coderre, Paul	20 00	
	do	615	Gervais, Jean B	20 00	
	do	964	Jubainville, Pierre	20 00	
	do	613	Massé, François	20 00	
	do	531	Mathon, Maurice	20 00	
	do	2037	Poulin, Joseph	20 00	
	do	3279	Morin, Victor		Services not proved.
	Ste. Rosalie	3234	Morin, Louis	20 00	
	do	2939	Savary, Augustin	20 00	

PENSIONS TO MILITIAMEN OF 1812-15.—*Continued.*

PROVINCE OF QUEBEC.—*Continued.*

Electoral District.	Post Office.	Number of Case.	Name of Militiaman.	Amount Paid.	Remarks.
				$ cts.	
BAGOT.—*Con*	St. Simon	819	Blais, Antoine	20 00	
	do	821	Delorme, Jean B		Dead.
	do	2148	Maheu, Joseph	20 00	
	do	820	Roby, Joseph	20 00	
	do	3214	Vandal, Léonard	20 00	
BEAUCE	Broughton	2492	Chatigny, Louis	20 00	
	do	2890	Hall, C. Henry	20 00	
	St. Elzear	968	Gregoire, Etienne	20 00	
	do	2172	Leblond, Joseph	20 00	
	St. Evariste	280	Regin, Jean B		Dead.
	do	279	Samson, Etienne	20 00	
	St. Ephrem	432	Poulin, Alexis	20 00	
	St. François	434	Rodrigue, Olivier	20 00	
	do	431	Mathieu, François	20 00	
	St. George	282	Dupuis, T		Dead.
	St. Joseph	281	Maheu, Charles	00	
	Ste. Marie	326	Bilodeau, Michel	20 00	
	do	1540	Greniér, François	20 00	
	do	327	Leclerc, Joseph	20 00	
	do	3037	Veilleux, Joseph	20 00	
	St. Vital de Lambton	1252	Belanger, Prisque	20 00	
	do	1253	Blouin, Antoine	20 00	
BELLECHASSE	Beaumont	134	Costin, Frederick	20 00	
	do	1864	Gauvreau, Joseph	20 00	
	Buckland	1652	Boutin, Simon	20 00	
	do	1653	Corriveau, Benoni	20 00	
	do	1654	Morin, Charles	20 00	
	St. Charles	1110	Marcoux, Pierre	20 00	
	do	1130	Leclerc, Joseph	20 00	

PENSIONS TO MILITIAMEN OF 1812-15.—*Continued.*

PROVINCE OF QUEBEC.—*Continued.*

Electoral District.	Post Office	Number of Case.	Name of Militiaman.	Amount Paid.	Remarks.
				$ cts	
BELLECHASSE......	St. Michel............	899	Fiset, Prisque.............	20 00	
	do	898	Fradet, Antoine...........	20 00	
	St. Gervais..........	1988	Audette, Marc............ ...	20 00	
	do	1656	Drapeau, Charles.........	20 00	
	do	1136	Isabelle, Guillaume......	20 00	
	do	3343	Tenguay, Raphael........	20 00	
	do	483	Turgeon, Guillaume.....	20 00	
	St. Raphael..........	1134	Bolduc, Jacques...........	20 00	
	do	125	Buteau, Louis..............	21 00	
	do	1131	Goulet, Jean..............	22 00	
	do	886	Ratté, Ignace	20 00	
	do	1137	Roby, André	20 00	
	St. Valier.......	759	Hoffman, Jean B...........	....	Dead.
BERTHIER.	Berthier.............	2203	Coutu, Jean B..............	20 00	
	do	2269	Delisle, Alexis.............	20 00	
	do	240	Guilbault, Hypolite.	20 00	
	do	2422	Lavalee, Paul.............	....	Dead.
	do	502	St. Arnault, Charles......	20 00	
	do	2415	Bellevalle, Pierre..........	20 00	
	do	3420	Mousseau, Alexis..........	....	Services not proved.
	Lanoraie.	673	Prazean, François.........	20 00	
	do	672	Caisse, Antoine.............	20 00	
	do	675	Desroslers, Alexir........	....	Dead.
	do	677	Pilon, J. Bte.	20 00	
	do	674	Robillard, Maurice.........	20 00	
	....	1926	Valois, Jean B.............	20 00	
	Lavaltrie............	2405	Ayet, Basile...............	20 00	
	do	990	Bourdon, Michel...........	....	Dead.
	do	973	Delisle, Pierre.............	20 00	

47

PENSIONS TO MILITIAMEN OF 1812-15.—*Continued.*

PROVINCE OF QUEBEC.—*Continued.*

Electoral District.	Post Office	Number Case.	Name of Militiaman.	Amount Paid.	Remarks.
				$ cts.	
BERTHIER.—*Con*	Lavaltrie............	961	Giguere, Claude............	20 00	
do	....	983	Lacombe, Joseph............	20 00	
do	....	970	Laporte, Charles............	20 00	
do	....	979	Lesage, Jean B............	20 00	
do	....	977	Morin, Joseph............	....	Dead.
do	....	973	Prud'homme, Louis.......	20 00	
do	....	1315	Renaud, Pierre............	20 00	
do	....	971	Rivet, Louis...............	20 00	
do	....	1614	Robillard, André............	20 00	
do	....	1314	Courcy, Benjamin.........	20 00	
St. Barthelomi......		244	Denommé, Alexis.........	20 00	
do	......	239	Gauthier, Amable.........	....	Dead.
do	......	2204	Guernon, François.......	20 00	
do	......	243	Savole, Ambroise.........	20 00	
do	......	241	Vilandré, Vital............	20 00	
St. Cuthbert.........		2202	Carpentier, Benjamin....	20 00	
do	....	2209	Chaussé Alexis............	....	Dead
do	....	3031	Généreux, Joseph.........	20 00	
do	....	2354	Sylvestre, Pierre............	20 00	
do	....	2590	Toupin, Michel............	20 00	
St. Gabriel.........		109	Brulé, Joseph	20 00	
do	....	1616	Courtemanche, Louis P.	20 00	
do	....	1258	Généreux, Ambroise.....	20 00	
do	......	110	Lanoie, Louis............	20 00	
St. Norbert.........		484	Boucher, Henri............	20 00	
do	....	114	Champagne, Joseph.......	20 00	
do	....	112	Frechette, Amable	20 00	
do	....	115	Robillard, Pierre.........	20 00	
do	....	111	Roy, François............	20 00	
do	....	113	Roy, Gabriel............	20 00	

PENSIONS TO MILITIAMEN OF 1812-15 —*Continued.*

PROVINCE OF QUEBEC.—*Continued.*

Electoral District.	Post Office	Number of Case.	Name of Militiaman.	Amount Paid.	Remarks.
				$ cts.	
BROME	Bolton	624	Hunt, John B	20 00	
	Brome	1102	Bedard, François	20 00	
	do	625	Schofelt, Thomas	20 00	
	Bromemere	430	Jones, Charles H	20 00	
	Knowlton	3156	Balls, James	20 00	
	do	2640	Daniels, Joseph	20 00	
	Farnham Centre	1574	Dell, George	20 00	
	Farnham East	2270	Cameron, Daniel	20 00	
	Sutton	1447	Schufelt, Joseph	20 00	Dead.
	do	3334	Best, Alexander	20 00	Services not proved.
CHAMBLY	Boucherville	1774	Benard, Jean B	20 00	
	ao	1776	Jodcin, Hippolyte	20 00	
	do	3284	Livernois, Felix	20 00	
	do	1775	Pariseau, Michel D	20 00	
	do	361	St. Onge, Jean B	20 00	
	do	3321	Valleé, Michel	20 00	
	do	3285	Sénécal, Paul	20 90	
	do	1205	Aubertin, Antoine	20 00	
	do	3286	Gervais, Theophile	20 00	Services not provec.
	do	3487	Bourdon, Fs. Antoine	20 00	Services not proved.
	Chambly (Basin)	259	Proteau, Nicholas	20 00	
	do	3393	Marcille, Antoine		On list for 1st July, 1877.
	Longueuil	8	Brechin, J. B	20 00	
	do	11	Birtz, Pierre	20 00	
	do	2115	Charron, François	20 00	
	do	2243	Fausse, Pierre		Dead.
	do	1690	Patenaude, Alexis	20 00	
	do	9	Phedi, Jean B	20 00	
	do	10	Sicotte, Constant	20 00	

PENSIONS TO MILITIAMEN OF 1812-15.—*Continued.*

PROVINCE OF QUEBEC.—*Continued.*

Electoral District.	Residence.	Number of Case.	Name of Militiaman.	Amount Paid.	Remarks.
				$ cts.	
CHAMBLY.—*Con*	Longueuil	2599	Trudeau, André	20 C0	
	do	2519	Viger, François B	20 00	
	d⁰	13	Cadieux, Joseph		Services not proved.
	c⁰	46	Richard Louis		Services not proved.
	St. Bas..s	1215	Racine, François		Dead.
	St. Bruno	053	Cadieux, François	20 00	
	do	2600	Paquin, Amable	20 00	
	do	1618	Protot, André	20 00	
	do	3401	St. André, Pierre		On list for 1st July, 1877.
	St. Hubert	731	Bouthiller, Alexis	20 00	
	do	12	Sabourin, Joseph	20 00	
	do	729	Vincent, Michel	20 00	
CHARLEVOIX	Bay St. Paul	881	Boi'y, Isaac	20 00	
	do	880	Fortin, Vital	20 00	
	do	879	Gagnon, Jacques	20 00	
	do	877	Lavoie, Oliver	20 00	
	do	878	Lavoie, Thomas	20 00	
	do	876	Pilote, Felix	20 00	
	do	882	Potvin Archange	20 00	
	do	883	Simard, Timothée	20 00	
	Eboulements	1257	Bergeron, Phillippe	20 00	
	do	1286	Gagnon, Felix	20 00	
	do	1285	Girard, Pierre	20 00	
	do	1917	Rheaume, Alexis	20 08	
	do	1283	Tremblay, Louis		Dead.
	do	3383	Bouchard, Ignace		On list for 1st July, 1877.
	Isle aux Cc dres	830	Gagnon, François	20 00	
	St. Agnès	408	Gagnon, Louis	20 00	
	St. Fidèle	404	Grenon, Joseph	20 00	

PENSIONS TO MILITIAMEN OF 1812-15.—*Continued.*

PROVINCE OF QUEBEC.—*Continued.*

Electoral District.	Residence.	Number of Case.	Name of Militiaman.	Amount Paid.	Remarks.
				$ cts.	
CHARLEVOIX—*Con*	St. Fidèle	405	Pilon, Nicholas	20 00	
	St. Frs. Xavier	1135	Neron, Alexis	20 00	
	St. Hilarion	2361	Tremblay, Pierre	20 00	
	St. Irenée	1295	Boivin, Elisé	20 00	
	do	1296	Fortin, Jacques	20 00	
	St. Urbain	437	Asselin, Jean B	20 00	
	do	436	Racine, Michel	20 00	
	do	435	Simard, Ulric	20 00	
CHAMPLAIN	Batiscan	1277	Gendron, Alexis	20 00	
	do	1274	Marchand, Joseph	20 00	
	d	1278	Moreau, Gabriel	20 00	
		940	Toupin, Joseph	20 00	
	Cap de la Magdeleine	2152	Dubord, Zenobie	20 00	
	do	2153	Lamothe, Joseph	20 00	
	do	2780	Montplaisir, Paschal	20 00	
	do	3085	St. Pierre, Clement		Dead.
	Champlain	2480	Dautigny, François X	20 00	
	Mort Carmel	1104	Drolet, Pierre	20 00	
	Ste. Anne de la P'de	452	Dalbec, François		Dead.
	do	1160	Godin, Louis	20 00	
	do	1157	Grimard, Joseph	20 00	
	do	1156	Lafleche, Olivier	20 00	
	do	1159	Laquerre, Hilaire	20 00	
	do	1155	Paré, Barthelemi	20 00	
	do	1154	Perrault, Louis	20 00	
	do	2566	Perrault, Dominique	20 00	
	do	1323	Tessier, François	20 00	
	do	1159	Williams, Joseph	20 00	

PENSIONS TO MILITIAMEN OF 1812-15.

PROVINCE OF QUEBEC.—Continued.

Electoral District.	Residence.	Number of Case.	Name of Militiaman.	Amount Paid.	Remarks.
				$ cts.	
CHAMPLAIN—Con	Ste. Genevieve.....	316	Baril, Francois	20 00	
	do	314	Cadotte, Jean B...........	....	Dead.
	do	311	Lefebvre, Nicholas........		Dead.
	do	313	Massicotte, Abraham	, 20 00	
	do	2859	Normandin, Pierre	20 00	
	do	315	Veillet, Jean B...........	20 00	
	do	3329	Allard, Francois..........	20 00	
	St. Maurice...........	1260	Brulé, Pierre.....	....	Dead.
	do	1281	Limoges, Louis........ ....:	20 00	
	do	1280	Page, Joseph.....	20 00	
	do	1259	Thibault, Pierre.....	20 00	
	St. Narcisse........	310	Baril, Joseph........	20 00	
	do	1649	Ratté, Charles..............	20 00	
	St. Prospère........	312	Massicotte, Augustin.....	....	No return.
	St. Stanislas........	409	Ayotte, François..	20 00	
	do	211	Caya, Clément.............	20 00	
	do	1163	Grimard, Modeste........ .	....	Dead.
	do	212	Lafontaine, Sifroi...........	20 00	
	do	2486	Lafontaine, Stanislas.....	....	Dead.
	do	1162	Massicotte, Jean B	20 00	
CHATEAUGUAY...	Chateauguay	1747	Boursier, Louis N	20 00	
	do	82	Dorais, Jean L......	20 00	
	do	1746	Monmillon, Louis	20 00	
	Ormstown...........	2414	Caron, Pierre	20 00	
	Russelltown	3391	Pagé, Benoit...............	....	Services not proved.
	St. J. Chrysostôme.	2550	Foucreau, François........	....	Dead.
	do ...	2536	Niquette, Jean B..	20 00	
	do ...:	2570	Provost, Alexis...........	....	Dead.
	St. Martine...........	2193	Brault, Vital...............	20 00	

PENSIONS TO MILITIAMEN OF 1812-15.—*Continued.*

PROVINCE OF QUEBEC.—*Continued.*

Electoral District.	Residence.	Number of Case.	Name of Militiaman.	Amount Paid.	Remarks.
				$ cts.	
CHATEAUGUAY ...	St. Martine.............	98	Clement, François	20 00	
	do	192	Cole, John........	20 00	
	do	2441	Duquet, Joachim...........	20 00	
	do	2618	Fournier, Pierre	....	Dead.
	do	1641	Legault, Pierre	20 00	
	do	2347	Lefebvre, Jean B..	....	Dead.
	do	1642	Mabeu, Antoine......	....	Dead.
	do	3377	Monette, Louis.............	20 00	
	do	2868	Varrain, François.........	20 00	
	St. Philomène......	3040	Hubardeau, Joseph	20 00	
	do	803	Loisel, Jean..................	20 00	
	do	73	Tremblay, Etienne........	20 00	
	St. Urbain...........	2010	Buteau, Nicholas..........	20 00	
	do	3150	Bessette, Joseph.	20 00	
	do	3038	Champagne, Antoine.....	20 00	
CHICOUTIMI	Bagotville.	540	Gendron, Jacques..........	20 00	
	do	976	Tremblay, François	20 00	
	do	1386	Harton, Ignace.............	20 00	
	do	1385	Laforge, François.........	20 00	
	Chicoutimi...........	2051	Boily, Jean B	....	Dead.
	Herbertville	2490	Gagné, Louis.....	20 00	
	Lac St. Jean..........	2394	Bluteau, Isidore......	....	Dead.
	St. Alexis	1387	Harvey, Joseph.............	20 00	
	St. Anne............	774	Duval, Hilaire.	20 00	
	St Paul.....	1427	Duchène, Jean B..........	....	Dead.
	Laterrlere...	1380	Singclais, Sauveur........	20 00	
	do	1390	Blackburn, Augustin.....	20 00	
	do	1287	Tremblay, Etienne........	20 00	

53

PENSIONS TO MILITIAMEN OF 1812-15.—Continued.

PROVINCE OF QUEBEC. —Continued.

Electoral District	Residence.	Number of Case.	Name of Militiaman.	Amount Paid.	Remarks.
				$ cts.	
COMPTON.	'tshire	577	Jackson, Peter		Services not proved.
	Robinson	3447	Barbeau, Amable		Services not proved.
	Sawyersville	1509	Rand, Arlemas D	20 00	
	Waterville	449	Germain, Jean D	20 00	
	Westbury	2060	Lothrop, Galen	20 00	
DORCHESTER.	Frampton	2171	Henderson, William	20 00	
	St. Anselme	2833	Garant, Jean	20 00	
	do	1989	Poulet, Charles	20 00	
	do	2008	Roy, Pierre	20 00	
	Ste. Claire	928	Lafontaine, Jacques		Dead.
	do	929	Lapointe, Charles	20 00	
	do	3212	Royer, Lazare V	20 00	
	Ste. Hénédine	1265	Bilodeau, Pierre	20 00	
	do	919	Roberge. Pierre		Dead.
	St. Isidore	927	Longchamp, Antoine	20 00	
	do	926	Patty, Antoine		Dead.
	do	2860	Roy, François	20 00	
	Ste. Marguerite	931	Chaloup, Michel	20 00	
	do	930	Roy, François	20 00	
	St. Malachie	2160	Henderson, Gilbert	20 00	
DRUMMOND.	Drummondville	2145	Metivier, André	20 00	
	Kingsey	3199	Babineau, Charles		Dead.
	do	1588	Cameron, Samuel	20 00	
	do	182	Cormier, Jean B	20 00	
	do	2001	Noel, Alexis		Dead.
	do	2959	Rousseau, Joseph,		Dead.
	do	3198	Vien, André	20 00	
	L'Avenir	306	Boisvert, Pierre	20 00	
	do	2588	Labonté, Louis		Dead.

PENSIONS TO MILITIAMEN OF 1812-15.—*Continued.*

PROVINCE OF QUEBEC.—*Continued.*

Electoral District.	Residence.	Number of Case.	Name of Militiaman.	Amount Paid.	Remarks.
				$ cts.	
DRUMMOND.—*Con.*	L'Avenir	305	Lepine, André	20 00	
	do	304	Leprohon, Joseph	20 00	
	do	764	Emoud, Antoine	20 00	
	St. Germain	2544	Fleury, Antoine	20 00	
	do	2922	Raiche, Antoine	20 00	
	St. Guillaume	908	Beauvais, Louis V	20 00	
	do	903	Belisle, Fra. X		Dead.
	do	904	Lambert, Louis	20 00	
	do	905	Vincent, Isaac	20 00	
	do	907	Doyon, Prisque		Dead.
	do	2931	Duguay, Antoine	20 00	
GASPÉ	Cap Chat	2508	Sergerie, St. Jore Firmin	20 00	
	St. Anne des Monts	2368	Levasseur, Augustin	20 00	
HOCHELAGA	Hochelaga	1520	Bourbonnière, Jean B		Dead.
	Longue Pointe.	1532	Hasinet, Antoine		Dead.
	do	3102	Brouiller, Joseph	20 00	
	do	1531	Decary, Hippolyte	20 00	
	do	1535	Jeannot, Prudent	20 00	
	Pte. aux Trembles	1472	Boyer, Torssaint	20 00	
	do	1471	Brouillet, Jean B	20 00	
	do	1493	Chalifoux, Jean B	20 00	
	do	1470	Chalifoux, Michel	20 00	
	do	1495	Jeannot, Antoine.	20 00	
	do	1491	Mouet François	20 00	
	Riv. des Prairies	2517	Bleau Joseph		Dead.
	do	2617	Cadieux, Joseph	20 00	
	do	2616	Cadieux, Jean B	20 00	
	do	2515	Fortin, Jean B	20 00	
	do	2621	Gosselin, Louis		Services not proved.

PENSIONS TO MILITIAMEN OF 1812-15.—*Continued.*

PROVINCE OF QUEBEC.—*Continued.*

Electoral District.	Residence.	Number of Case.	Name of Militiaman.	Amount Paid.	Remarks.
				$ cts	
HOCHELAGA.—*Con*	Sault aux Recol-lets.	90	Labranche, Jean L........	20 00	
	do ...	1697	Pesant, François..........	20 00	
	St. Jean Baptiste..	799	Jubainville, Pierre........	20 00	
	do ..	2155	Dagenais, François........	20 00	
	do ..	573	Lapierre, François........	20 00	
	do ..	2413	Rodier, Joseph.....	20 00	
	do ..	2620	Viau, A...................		Services not proved.
	Tannery West......	133	Bourdon, Joseph..........	20 00	
	do	1907	Langevin, Jacques........	20 00	
	do	291	Wilscamp, John...........	20 00	
	do	292	Rolland, Lenoir G........		Dead.
	do	550	Legault, Joseph...........	20 00	
	do	3307	Deschambault, Nicholas	20 00	
	do	3347	Gervais, Alexis....	20 00	
HUNTINGDON	Covey Hill..........	2861	O'Neil, Hugh	20 00	
	Dundee..............	1792	Ashburn, John............	20 00	
	Franklin Centre ...	3418	Longway, Joseph		Services not proved.
	Helena...............	2571	Primeau, Jean B..	20 00	
	Hemingford..........	246	Catman, Pierre.......	20 00	
	do	2226	Reneault, Pierre		No return.
	do	245	Robert, François..........	20 00	
	do	3256	Scriver, William..	20 00	
	St. Anicet	1883	Langlois, Benjamin.		Dead.
	St. Regis.............	3180	Kansitatsika, Kor	20 00	
	do	3179	Hemlock, Jacob...........	20 00	
	Starnsboro'..........	2105	Beauregard, Gabriel......	20 00	
	do	2030	Gaboriault, Joseph.......	20 00	
	do	2852	Gervais, Constant	20 00	
	do	2031	Gibeau, François	20 00	
	do	2919	Mitivier, Jean B..........	20 00	

PENSIONS TO MILITIAMEN OF 1812-15.—*Continued.*

PROVINCE OF QUEBEC.—*Continued.*

Electoral District.	Post Office.	Number of Case.	Name of Militiaman.	Amount Paid	Remarks.
				$ cts.	
IBERVILLE	Henryville	1362	Grenier, Pierre	20 00	
	do	813	Guérin, Guillaume	20 00	
	do	2173	Lecuyer, Pierre	20 00	
	do	2057	Courchene, Charles	20 00	
	do	2258	Magnant, Joseph	20 00	
	Iberville	1353	Bessette, Julien	30 00	
	do	1738	Bousquet, Hippolyte	20 00	
	do	1955	Corriveau, Charles	20 00	
	do	3339	Granger, Jean B	20 00	
	do	522	Joubert, Joseph	20 00	
	do	2090	Larocque, Louis	20 00	
	do	2082	Maintesse, Louis.	20 00	
	do	3374	Massé, François	20 00	
	do	789	Menard, Ambroise	20 00	
	do	2532	Lessard. Louis	20 00	
	do	3372	Choquette, Pierre		Services not proved.
	Mount Johnson	3121	Jasmin, Noel	20 00	
	Sabrevois	2330	Jones, Thomas	20 00	
	St. Alexandre	697	Dalpé, Noel	20 00	
	do	812	Monat, Joseph	20 00	
	do	696	Nerbonne, Jacques	20 00	
	do	1933	Robert, Louis		Dead.
	do	3282	Lamothe, Pierre	20 00	
	Ste. Brigide	1047	Bougrette, Jean L	20 00	
	do	3203	Jourdain, Joachim	20 00	
	do	1193	Lemaire, Michel	20 00	
	do	3390	Beauregard, Pierre		Services not proved.
	St. Gregoire	2284	Bessette, Edouard	20 00	
	do	2420	Choquette, Jean B	20 00	

PENSIONS TO MILITIAMEN OF 1812-15.—*Continued.*

PROVINCE OF QUEBEC.—*Continued.*

Electoral District.	Residence.	Number of Case.	Name of Militiaman.	Amount Paid.	Remarks.
				$ cts.	
IBERVILLE.—*Con...*	St. Gregoire	2322	Desrochers, Pierre	20 00	
	do	2510	Hébert, Jean B	20 00	
	do	2511	Laperche, Isaac.............	20 00	
	do	2283	Patenaude, François	20 00	
	St. Sebastien	2060	Doivin, Michel	20 00	
	do	2061	Breau, Pierre	20 00	
	do	2512	Carpentier, Louis	20 00	
	do	52	Martin, Henry	....	Dead.
JACQUES CAR-TIER	do	2059	Pierre, Broulllette	....	Services not proved.
	Isle Bizard	3092	Trepanier, Jacques.........	20 00	
	Lachine	848	Boileau, Athanaso.........	20 00	
	do	1403	Crepeau, Jean B	20 00	
	do	208	McNaughton, Donald....	20 00	
	do	850	Vallières, Pierre	....	Dead.
	Pointe Claire.........	801	Pilon, André.............	20 00	
	do	800	Trottier, J. B......	20 00	
	do	3392	Perrier, Antoine.............	....	Services not proved.
	St. Anne (Bout de l'Isle.............	773	Gauthier, Bernardin......	20 00	
	do	2607	Lalonde, Luc.............	20 00	
	do	2121	Lebuies, Augustin	20 00	
	do	752	Perrier, Pierre......	....	Dead.
	Ste. Geneviève......	128	Brisebois, François	20 00	
	do	131	Martin, Joseph.............	20 00	
	St. Laurent.............	1526	Boudrias, Louis.............	20 00	
	do	1527	Gauthier, Antoine.........	20 00	
	do	2416	Lebeau, Jacques	20 00	
	do	2627	Martin, Pierre.............	20 00	
	do	1528	Malette, Jean B.............	20 00	
	do	2925	Tarte, Luc	20 00	

PENSIONS TO MILITIAMEN OF 1812-15.—*Continued.*

PROVINCE OF QUEBEC.—*Continued.*

Electoral District.	Residence.	Number of Case.	Name of Militiaman.	Amount Paid.	Remarks.
				$ cts.	
JOLIETTE............	Joliette..............	2412	Beaudoin, Frs..............	20 00	
	do	2894	Beauregard, J. B.	20 00	
	do	76	Beauchamp, Paul........	20 00	
	do	2408	Forrest, Joseph	20 00	
	do	2893	Lacoste, Francois........	20 00	
	do	2411	Lavigne, J. B...............	20 00	
	do	2937	Leprohon, Philippe	....	Dead.
	do	2406	Prudhomme, Joseph	20 00	
	do	336	Bonin, Jean B..............	20 00	
	do	2022	Michaud, Henry.	20 00	
	Kildare	2523	Gilbert, Jean B.............	20 00	
	St. Côme	40	Melançon. Joseph	20 20	Dead.
	do	41	Prud'homme, Joseph.....	....	
	St. Elizabeth	335	Durand, Joseph............	20 00	
	do	3032	Guilbault, Antoine........	....	Dead.
	do	334	Latour, Pierre........	20 00	
	do	1612	Levêsque............	20 00	
	do	337	Sarazin, Joseph............	....	Dead.
	do	504	Thibodeau, Joseph	....	Dead.
	St. Felix de Valois	1363	Aubin, Alexis	20 00	
	do ...	2475	Joly, Ardouin ....'......	20 00	
	do ...	2126	Letourneau, Alexis........	20 00	
	do ...	189	Manseau, Charles..........	20 00	
	do ...	2433	St. George, Emmanuel ..	....	Dead.
	St. Jean de Matha.	1590	Racette, Joseph...	20 00	
	do ...	2897	Roy, Jean B...............	20 00	
	Ste. Melanie........	2410	Brault, Paul..............	20 00	
	St. Paul............	2522	Rivest, François...........	20 00	
	do	1667	Portelance, Basile........	20 00	

PENSIONS TO MILITIAMEN OF 1812-16.—Continued.

PROVINCE OF QUEBEC.—Continued.

Electoral District.	Post Office.	Number of Case.	Name of Militiaman.	Amount Paid.	Remarks.
				$ cts.	
JOLIETTE.—Con....	St. Paul...............	2895	Deziel, Joseph...............		Services not proved.
	St. Thomas.........	333	Boucher, Pierre............	20 00	
	do	2614	Coutu, Basile-............	20 00	
	do	1915	Coutu, François..........	20 00	
	do	332	Desrosiers, Ambroise.....	20 00	
	do	1589	Langlois, François........	20 00	
KAMOURASKA......	Rivière Ouelle......	149	Emond, Hyacinthe........	20 00	
	do	146	Levêsque, Paschal........		Dead.
	do	162	Ouellet, Charles..........		Dead.
	St. Alexandre......	1237	Beaupré, Noel.............	20 00	
	do	1225	Chenard, Louis	20 00	
	do	1236	Gagné, Paschal	20 00	
	Ste. Anne............	823	Berubé, Jean B.............	20 00	
	do	147	Bourgelas. Maurice.......	20 00	
	do	148	L'Italien, François........	20 00	
	do	150	Sirois, Jean	20 00	
	St. André	1224	Pelletier, Etienne........		Dead.
	do	1063	Soucy, Michel.............	20 00	
	do	824	Dubé, Honoré.............	20 00	
	Ste. Hélène..........	939	Charest, Michel	20 00	
	St. Pacôme...........	145	Boucher, Jean D...........	20 00	
	do	138	Leclerc, Jean Bte........	20 00	
	do	139	Levêsque, Eloi.............	20 00	
	do	144	Perreault, Isaie............	20 00	
	St. Paschal...........	153	Ouellet, André.............	20 00	
	do	151	Ouellet, J. Charles........	20 00	
LAPRAIRIE......	Caughnawaga......	3184	Anewarion, Louis.........	20 00	
	do	3186	Anioken, Jean...	20 00	
	do	2726	Aubry, François...........		Left limits.

PENSIONS TO MILITIAMEN OF 1812-15.—*Continued.*

PROVINCE OF QUEBEC.—*Continued.*

Electoral District.	Post Office.	Number of Case.	Name of Militiaman.	Amount Paid.	Remarks.
				$ cts.	
L.APRAIRIE.—*Con.*	Caughnawaga	508	Champagne, Louis	20 00	
	do	3168	Kasrkete, Fra	20 00	
	do	3187	Shakokenni, Pierre	20 00	
	do	3181	Sakoiatliosta, Joseph	20 00	
	do	3183	Sonorese, Nathias	20 00	
	do	3185	Shobalio, Jacques	20 00	
	Laprairie	2921	Brassard, Pierre	20 00	
	do	2196	Duraucceu, Pierre		Dead.
	do	2647	Niding, J. B	20 00	
	do	3080	Poupart, Alexis	20 00	
	do	2006	Poupart, Jacques	20 00	
	do	2649	Rackenpack, Paul	20 00	
	do	2648	Rousseau, J. B	20 00	
	do	3322	Brousseau, Jacques		Services not proved.
	St. Constant	3310	Barbeau, Jacques	20 00	
	do	2991	Letourneau, Joseph	20 00	
	do	3294	Lefort, Amable	20 00	
	St. Isidore	2621	Dourdeau, Ignace	20 00	
	do	2848	Brosseau, Louis	20 00	
	do	2460	Denault, J. B		Dead.
	do	1376	Gervais, Augustin	20 00	
	do	2521	Gervais, François	20 00	
	do	2973	Kingley, Paul	20 00	
	do	2525	Perras, Simon	20 00	
	do	3336	Gervais, Charles	20 00	
	St. Jacques	1789	Daignenault, Antoine	20 00	
	St. Philippe	135°	Desnoyers, André	20 00	
	do	782	Gagnier, Pierre	20 00	
	do	2375	Longtin, Jean B		No return.
	do	3490	Denoyers, Antoine D		On list for 1st July, 1877.

PENSIONS TO MILITIAMEN OF 1812-15.—*Continued.*

PROVINCE OF QUEBEC.—*Continued.*

Electoral District.	Post Office.	Number of Case.	Name of Militiaman.	Amount Paid.	Remarks.
				$ cts.	
L'ASSOMPTION	Lacheuaie	2428	Lamoureux, Jacques......	20 00	
	L'Assomption.......	235	Brien, Joseph Ed...........	20 00	
	do	87	Chaput, Joseph	20 00	
	(῾	86	Chevandière, Pierre......	20 00	
	do	828	Chevigny, Jean B	20 00	
	do	2956	Christin, Jean B...........	20 00	
	do	106	Gauthier, François........	....	Dead.
	do	236	Malo, Joachim...............	20 00	
	do	2961	Morin, Sulpice	20 00	
	d5	107	Quesnel, Antoine..........	20 00	
	L'Epiphanie	104	St. Louis, Charles	20 00	
	Mascouche.............	2881	Beauchamp, Jean.	20 00	
	do	3355	Corbeil, François..........	20 00	
	St. Lin...............	238	Brabant, Paul...............	20 00	
	do	234	Ethier, Abraham	20 00	
	do ...."....	1309	Fournier, Michel...........	20 00	
	do	232	Gueri-Dumont, Joseph...	20 00	
	do	2481	Roy, Alexis	20 00	
	do	237	Therien, Louis	....	Dead.
	do	3154	Varain, Pierre..............	20 00	
	St. Roch...............	2483	Deziel André.	20 00	
	do	3152	Dulpe, Joseph	20 00	
	do	2539	Piootte, Augustin..........	20 00	
	do	2531	Lebeau, Pierre.............	20 00	
	St. Sulpice...	105	Pelletier, François........	20 00	
	do	3250	Perrault, Pierre C.........	20 00	
LAVAL.....	Ste. Dorothée.......	2244	Galipeau, Laurent..........	20 00	
	do	2245	Theoret, Eustache	20 00	
	St. Francis de Sales	225	Lemay, Hyacinthe.	20 00	

PENSIONS TO MILITIAMEN OF 1812-15.—*Continued.*

PROVINCE OF QUEBEC.—*Continued.*

Electoral District.	Residence.	Number of Case.	Name of Militiaman.	Amount Paid.	Remarks.
				$ cts.	
LAVAL.—*Con.*	St. Martin	1108	Barbe, Louis	20 00	
	do	2025	Bergeron, Guillaume		Dead.
	do	2032	Beautrain, François	20 09	
	do	2161	Gerard, Joseph	20 00	
	do	450	Laurin, Paul	20 00	
	do	3377	Monette, Louis	20 00	
	do	721	Valade, François		Dead.
	do	722	Patry, François	20 00	
	do	3400	Lavoie, Martin		Services not proved.
	Ste. Rose	392	Dumoulin, Joseph	20 00	
	do	391	Gascon, François		Dead.
	do	2303	Miller, Jean		Dead.
	St. Vincent de Paul	013	Charbonneau, Joseph	20 00	
	do	644	Loyer, Louis	20 00	
LEVIS	Lévis	1318	Beaulieu, Edouard	20 00	
	do	1091	Fournier, Germain	20 00	
	do	947	Drapeau, Joseph	20 00	
	do	894	Cameron, Antoine	20 00	
	do	957	Dion, Frs. X	20 00	
	do	946	Drouin, Amable	20 00	
	do	774	Montminy, Michel	20 00	
	St Henri	1986	Degin, Joseph		Dead.
	do	1583	Belleau, Pierre	20 00	
	do	1785	Bilodeau, Jean	20 00	
	do	1393	Coulombe, Antoine	20 00	
	do	854	Couture, Jean	20 00	
	do	1830	Degourdelle, Pierre	20 00	
	do	1755	Gagné, Louis		Dead
	do	1790	Jolicœur, Thomas	20 00	

PENSIONS TO MILITIAMEN OF 1812-15.—Continued.

PROVINCE OF QUEBEC.—Continued.

Electoral District.	Residence.	Number of Case.	Name of Militiaman.	Amount Paid.	Remarks.
				$ cts.	
LEVIS.—Continued.	St. Henri	1087	Lecours, Joseph		No return.
	do	2505	Ruel, Jean		Dead.
	St. Jean Chrysostome.	1918	Savard, François	20 00	
	St. Joseph	982	Brochu, François	20 00	
	do	930	Bourget, Louis	20 00	
	do	414	Charbonneau, Charles		Dead.
	do	2507	Letourneau, Benoit J		Dead.
	do	267	Montminy, Etienne	20 00	
	do	951	Noel, Jean Bte..	20 00	
	do	2151	Patry, François	20 00	
	do	949	Ruel, François	20 00	
	do	669	Pellerin, Damase	20 00	
	St. Lambert	1756	Morin, Louis	20 00	
	St. Nicholas	2806	Dion, Joseph	20 00	
	do	339	Dubois, Noel	20 00	
	do	1256	Dupéré, Etienne	20 00	
	do	2038	Fréchette, F. X	20 00	
	do	1255	Fréchette, Michel	20 00	
	St. Romuald	1079	Bissonnette, Pierre	20 00	
	do	1076	Denis, Etienne	20 00	
	do	1077	Hoart, François	20 00	
	do	1078	Munro, P. Basile		Dead.
L'ISLET	L'Islet	1352	Berger, Guillaume	20 00	
	do	1392	Despré, Marcel		Dead.
	do	1436	Dessaint, François J		Dead.
	do	1331	Lamarre, François	20 00	
	do	1168	Morin, Joseph	20 00	
	St. Jean, Port Joly	214	Bourgault, François	20 00	
	do	154	Harton, Joseph	20 00	

PENSIONS TO MILITIAMEN OF 1812-15.—*Continued.*

PROVINCE OF QUEBEC.—*Continued.*

Electoral District.	Post Office.	Number of Case.	Name of Militiaman	Amount Paid.	Remarks.
				$ cts.	
L'ISLET.—*Con*	do	142	Ouellet, Alexis		Dead.
	St. Roch	143	Castonguay, Joseph	20 00	
	do	141	St Amant, Abraham	20 00	
LOTBINIERE	Beaurivage	137?	Sylvain, Joseph	20 00	
	do	1262	Gonthier, Pierre	20 00	
	Leclercville	?2	Perusse, Luc	20 00	
	do	23	Brisson, Auguste	20 00	
	Lotbinière	428	Augé, Louis	20 00	
	do	601	Perusse, Louis	20 00	
	do	608	Boudreau, Olivier	20 00	
	Ste. Agathe	2083	Plante, Pierre	20 00	
	St. Antoine	546	Jacquet, François	20 00	
	do	551	Colombe, Antoine	20 00	
	do	554	Noel, Joseph	20 00	
	do	552	Noel, Jern B	20 00	
	do	545	Rousseau, Pierre	20 00	
	do	553	L'Ainé, Luc	20 00	
	St. Appolinaire	544	Rousseau, Benjamin	20 00	
	Ste. Croix	2176	Bergeron, Augustin	20 00	
	do	1094	Boisvert, Jean B	20 00	
	do	1095	Laroche, Charles	20 00	
	do	1096	Monfette, Antoine	20 00	
	St. Edouard	1145	Terrien, Joseph	20 00	
	do	1144	Blanchet, A. J	20 00	
	do	1146	St. Onge, Louis	20 00	
	St. Flavien	1662	Côté, Etienne	20 00	
	do	1661	Côté, Jean B	20 00	
	do	1660	Hamel, Pierre	20 00	
	St. Gilles	777	Wagner, Jean B	20 00	
	St Jean Deschaillons	1865	Maillot, Modeste		No return.

65

PENSIONS TO MILITIAMEN OF 1812-15.—*Continued.*

PROVINCE OF QUEBEC.—*Continued.*

Electoral District.	Post Office.	Number of Case.	Name of Militiaman.	Amount Paid.	Remarks.
				$ cts.	
MASKINONGE	Hunterstown	955	Elliot, Joseph	20 00	
	do	455	Valiere, Joseph	20 00	
	Maskinongé	3268	Durand, François	20 00	
	do	468	Jolette, François		No return.
	do	471	Labrèche, Medar D	20 00	
	do	469	Larose, Louis	20 00	
	do	472	Lebrun, Louis	20 00	
	do	2095	Marineau, François	20 00	
	do	415	Cloutier, Pierre		No return.
	do	3351	Grenier, Louis	20 00	
	do	467	Vannsse, Pierre		Services not proved.
	Rivière du Loup	520	Baribeau, Augustin	20 00	
	do	475	Carle, Joseph	20 00	
	do	479	Damphousse Amable	20 00	
	do	481	Desaulniers, Alexis	20 00	
	do	1617	Livernoche, Joseph	20 00	
	do	476	Loranger, Jean B	20 00	
	do	478	Paillé, Regis	20 00	
	do	477	Prat .nçois	20 00	
	do	480	Roy, François	20 00	
	do	2985	Voisard, François	20 00	
	St. Didace	2293	Juneau, Louis		Dead.
	do	3116	Laprade, Basile	20 00	
	St. Léon	454	Allard, Marc	20 00	
	do	1207	Lafleur, Pierre	20 00	
	do	456	Laperrière, Jean B	20 00	
	St. Justin	2271	Ayotte, François	20 00	
	do	1087	Clement, Louis	20 00	
	do	1095	Gagnon, Pierre	20 00	

PEFSIONS TO MILITIAMEN OF 1812-15.—*Continued.*

PROVINCE OF QUEBEC.—*Continued.*

Electoral District.	Post Office.	Number of Case.	Name of Militiaman.	Amount Paid.	Remarks.
				$ cts.	
MASKINONGÉ-*Con.*	St. Justin	473	Heroux, Michel	20 00	
	do	1088	Morin, Joseph	20 00	
•	do	1089	Perreault, Pierre	20 00	
	do	3115	Sicard, Joseph	20 00	
	do	1086	Roy, Joseph	20 00	
	do	3293	Fleury, Isidore		Services not proved.
	Ste. Ursule	465	Leclerc, Alexis	20 00	
	do	482	Picard, Joseph		Dead.
	do	460	Thibaudeau, Jean	20 00	
MEGANTIC	Lyster	660	Denis, Etienne	20 00	
	Somerset	161	Roux, Antoine	20 00	
	do	160	McCrae, Alexander	20 00	
	Ste. Julie	96	Lepage, Jean	20 00	
	do	92	Cö , Louis	20 00	
	St. Ferdinand	155	Binei, Pierre	20 00	
	do	156	Côté, Joseph	20 00	
	do	156	Hemond, Jean		Dead.
	Ste. Sophie	2572	Belliveau, Joseph	20 00	
	do	600	L'Enseigne, Augustin	20 00	
MISSISQUOI	Bedford	2587	Powers, George	20 00	
	do	3011	Resher, Joseph	20 00	
	Cowansville	1446	Humphry, Peter		Services not proved.
	Clarenceville	367	Beerworth, Henry	20 00	
	do	3367	Brown, Andrew	20 00	
	do	2137	Derrick, William	20 00	
	do	766	Derrick, Anthony	20 00	
	do	771	Emerick, Henry	20 00	
	do	872	Johnson, George W	20 00	
	do	767	Scott, William	20 00	

PENSIONS TO MILITIAMEN OF 1812-15.—*Continued.*

PROVINCE OF QUEBEC.—*Continued.*

Electoral District.	Post Office.	Number of Case.	Name of Militiaman.	Amount Paid.	Remarks.
				$ cts.	
MISSISQUOI.—*Con.*	Clarenceville........	2135	Sco.t, Thomas........	20 00	
	do	2136	Suxard, Felix............	20 00	
	Dunham......	2817	Wales, John D............	20 00	
	do	1342	Roy, Charles......	20 00	
	do	1923	Poulette, Joseph............	20 00	
	Farnham (West)...	1042	Allard, François..	20 00	
	do	2569	Barabé, Peter........	20 00	
	do	2568	Dismillon, Hippolyte......	20 00	
	do	2520	Davignon, Joseph...... ..	20 00	
	do	2566	Deslauriers, Michel........	20 00	
	do	1101	Riendeau, Antoine........	20 00	
	do	3034	Surprenant, Jean........	20 00	
	do	1105	Robidoux, Etienne........	20 00	
	do	2942	Welsh, Archelaus........	....	Services not. proved.
	Freligsburg........	3254	Etu, Alexis	20 00	
	Malmaison...	2970	Duquette, François........	20 00	
	do	1568	Goyett·, Joseph........	....	Dead.
	do	1341	Lange, Théodore............	20 00	
	do	1804	Larochelle, Michel........	20 00	
	do	18	L'Homme, Joseph	20 00	
	Nutt's Corners......	1341	Drew, James.	20 00	
	Philipsburg	55	Best, John............	20 00	
	do	1337	Luke, Jacob V............	00	
	do	1340	Moore, Hiram............	20 00	
	Pigeon Hill	3312	Picard, Pierre............	20 00	
	do	1573	Sornborger, John....	....	Dead.
	do	2962	McDonald, John	20 00	
	Pike River............	2058	Godreau, Joseph	20 00	
	do	2062	Charland Joseph........	20 00	

PENSIONS TO MILITIAMEN OF 1812 15.—*Continued.*

PROVINCE OF QUEBEC.—*Continued.*

Electoral District.	Post Office.	Number of Case.	Name of Militiaman.	Amount Paid.	Remarks.
				$ cts.	
MISSISQUOI.—*Con.*	Stanbridge	1343	Pratt, Theodore	20 00	
	de	1339	Traver, Philip	20 00	
	do	3301	Breton, Pierre		Services not proved.
	Sweetsburg	91	Basinet, Toussaint	20 00	
	do	2628	Bigelow, Horace	20 00	
	do	2344	Corrivèau, Charles		Services not proved.
	St. Armand	54	Boomhover, Jacob	20 00	
	do	2630	Holden, Arthur		Dead.
	do	1575	Holstapple, John	20 00	
	do	1578	Primerman, Peter	20 00	
	do	53	Salisbury, Henry	20 00	
	do	1336	Smith, John	20 00	
	do	1580	Sornborger, Jeremiah	20 00	
	do	2445	Wood, Joseph	20 00	
	do	2969	Higgins, Oram	20 00	
	St. Thomas	2207	Derrick, Henry		Dead.
	do	2134	Williams, Isaac	20 00	
MONTCALM	St. Alexis	1209	Beaudry, Toussaint	20 00	
	do	556	Fournier, Pierre		Dead.
	do	1208	Ratelle, Nicholas		Dead.
	do	3227	Beaudry, Joseph	20 00	
	St. Calixte	301	Brunet, Jean B	20 00	
	do	303	Imbault, Amable	20 00	
	do	302	Leclerc, François		Dead.
	do	300	Thienlle, J. Bte		Dead.
	do	3288	Chaput, Antoine		Services not proved.
	St. Esprit	3209	Soulière, Jean B	20 00	
	do	3210	Gauthier, Frs	20 00	
	do	3153	Leclaire, Antoine	20 00	

PENSIONS TO MILITIAMEN OF 1812-15.—*Continued.*

PROVINCE OF QUEBEC.—*Continued.*

Electoral District.	Post Office.	Number of Case.	Name of Militiaman.	Amount Paid.	Remarks.
				$ cts.	
MONTCALM.—*Con.*	St. Esprit..........	394	Sivignie, François.........	20 00	
	do	3207	Rochon, Jean B............	20 00	
	St. Jacques.	1820	Langlois, Jean B...........	20 00	
	do	1818	Lemay, François	20 00	
	do	2021	Legaré, Pierre	20 00	
	do	1823	Maheu, Michel.......................	....	Dead.
	do	1819	Marion, Joseph.............	20 00	
	do	1824	Melançon, David...........	20 00	
	do	1817	Richard, François.........	20 00	
	do	2896	Riopel, Joseph	20 00	
	do	1821	Rivet, Jean B	....	Dead.
	do	3242	Brisson, Ambrolse..........	20 00	
	Ste. Jelienne	1321	Beauchamp, Jean B.......	....	Dead.
	do	1342	Pelletier, Antoine.........	20 00	
	do	818	Rivais, Charles	20 00	
	do	2278	Collin, François...	20 00	
	do	3397	Ferron, Paul...................	....	Services not proved.
	St. Liguori	1825	Brisson, Jean B	....	Dead.
	do	1855	Caisse, Pierre.............	20 00	
	do	1824	Lanouo, Antoine	....	Dead.
	do	1329	Rivais, Alexis...............	20 00	
MONTMAGNY	Berthier.....	1859	Carbonneau, Joseph......	20 00	
	do	1860	Carbonneau, Jacques. ...	20 00	
	do	1861	Ratté, Laurent...............	20 00	
	do	1862	Blais, Laurent.............	20 00	
	Cap St. Ignace......	1708	Pelletier, Celestin.........	20 00	
	St. François	1250	Gendron, Laurent..........	20 00	
	St. Thomas	1502	Chevrette, Bernard..	20 00	
	do	1501	Fortier, Pierre........	20 00	

PENSIONS TO MILITIAMEN OF 1812-15.—*Continued.*

PROVINCE OF QUEBEC.—*Continued.*

Electoral District.	Post Office.	Number of Case.	Name of Militiaman	Amount Paid.	Remarks.
				$ cts.	
MONTMAGNY-*Con.*	St. Thomas............	1428	Fournier, Thomas.........	20 00	
	do	1429	Gaudreau, Antoine D....	20 00	
	do	896	Mathurin, Jean B.........	....	Dead.
	do	1500	Lacombe, Louis...........	20 00	
MONTMORENCY....	Chateau Richer.....	1130	Gravel, Simon...........	20 00	
	do	756	Lefrançois, Pierre.........	20 00	
	L'Ange Gardien...	2026	Laberge, Charles.........	20 00	
	do ...	3105	Vezina, Louis...........	20 00	
	Ste. Anne	1463	Bacon, Etienne...........	20 00	
	do	168	Mercier, Augustin........	20 00	
	do	2503	Mercier, François	20 00	
	do	294	Paré, Etienne............	20 00	
	do	2339	Simard, Basile	20 00	
	St. Famille, I.O ...	659	Paradis, Ignace	20 00	
	St. François, I.O...	1541	Gagné, Louis	20 00	
	do ...	758	Gagnon, Pierre	20 00	
	do ...	967	Pepin, Joseph	20 00	
	St. Jean, I.O.........	757	Blouin, Emery	....	Dead.
	do	1129	Gagnon, François	20 00	
	do	3	Labrecque, Joseph	20 00	
	do	1542	Laverdière, Jean B.	20 00	
	do	617	Pâquet, Pierre	20 00	
	St. Joachim	1015	Gagnon, Simon	20 00	
	St. Laurent, I.O ...	740	Coulombe, Ambroise	20 00	
	do ...	741	L'Abbé, Jacques	20 00	
	do ...	2132	Ruel, Antoine..	20 00	
	St. Tite des Caps ..	968	Bedard, Pierre............	20 00	
	do ...	966	Simard, Germain..........	20 00	

PENSIONS TO MILITIAMEN OF 1812-15.—*Continued.*

PROVINCE OF QUEBEC.—*Continued.*

Electoral District.	Post Office.	Number of Cases.	Name of Militiamen.	Amount Paid.	Remarks.
				$ cts.	
MONTREAL	Montreal	420	Allard, Charles		No return.
	do	1451	Amyot, Jean B	20 00	
	do	2964	Amyrauld, François	20 00	
	do	2622	Barré, Nicholas	20 00	
	do	176	Beaucaire, Joseph	20 00	
	do	784	Beauchamp, François	20 00	
	do	2040	Belanger, Prisque	20 00	
	do	1334	Belec, Louis		No return.
	do	3052	Birtz, Etienne	20 00	
	do	47	Blanchet, Etienne	20 00	
	do	2840	Bloudin, Joseph	20 00	
	do	2071	Boivin, Antoine	20 00	
	do	783	Bouchard, Jean	20 00	
	do	2584	Bouchard, Jean B.		No return.
	do	2376	Boudrias, Jean B.	20 00	
	do	1454	Bourgeault, Pierre	20 00	
	do	1604	Bousquet, Basile V	20 00	
	do	2381	Bouvelle, François	20 00	
	do	2913	Bouvier, Michel	20 00	
	do	21	Boyer, Benjamin		No return.
	do	7	Brodeur, Augustin	20 00	
	do	2629	Brown, Elakam	20 00	
	do	178	Cardinal, Joseph	20 00	
	do	3244	Carrier, Jacques	20 00	
	do	1452	Carpenter, Jean B	20 00	
		33	Corbeil, P : rs	10 00	
	do	1879	Crepeau, Jean B		No return.
	do	982	Daragon, Antoine	20 00	
	do	561	Dorval, Joseph	20 00	

PENSIONS TO MILITIAMEN OF 1812-15.—*Continued.*

PROVINCE OF QUEBEC.—*Continued.*

Electoral District.	Post Office.	Number of Case.	Name of Militiaman.	Amount Paid.	Remarks.
				$ cts.	
MONTREAL.—*Con..*	Montreal	1104	Dufaut, Augustin	20 00	
	do	2496	Dufresne, Paul	20 00	
	do	2476	Dumesnil, Charles	20 00	
	do	74	Dumoulin, François	20 00	
	do	3332	Favreau, Joseph	20 00	
	do	2304	Gadoury, Joseph	20 00	
	do	2604	Galipeau, Alexis	20 00	
	do	411	Garicpy, Pierre	20 00	
	do	2390	Garneau, Alexis		No return.
	do	2398	Gervais, Antoine		No return.
	do	2024	Gibeau, Joseph		No return.
	do	116	Goddu, Toussaint	20 00	
	do	371	Guimond, Antoine	20 00	
	do	3323	Idler, Ernest	20 00	
	do	2104	Jarret, Louis	20 00	
	do	1794	Jobin, Joseph		No return.
	do	45	Labelle, François		No return.
	do	574	Labelle, Charles		No return.
	do	275	Labelle, Charles	20 00	
	do	720	Labranche, Louis	20 00	
	do	2041	Lafleur, Jacques	20 00	
	do	3043	Lanthier, Louis		No return.
	do	2036	Latrimouile, Jean M	20 00	
	do	2144	Lauzon, Michel	20 00	
	do	3357	Lavoie, François		No return.
	do	2811	Lebuis, Louis	20 00	
	do	1121	Lemai, François	20 00	
	do	1384	Lessard, George	20 00	
	do	1737	Marois, Pierre	20 00	

PENSIONS OF MILITIAMEN OF 1812-15.—*Continued.*

PROVINCE OF QUEBEC.—*Continued.*

Electoral District.	Post Office.	Number of Case.	Name of Militiaman.	Amount Paid.	Dead.
				$ cts.	
MONTREAL.—*Con.*	Montreal	3010	Meloche, François		No return.
	do	1840	Patenaud, Joseph	20 00	
	do	2318	Pâquet, François	20 00	
	do	1603	Pilon, Pierre	20 00	
	do	2097	Plourde, André	20 00	
	do	331	Richard, Jean B	20 00	
	do	72	Rottot, Pierre		Dead.
	do	24	St. Jean, François		No return.
	do	1880	Thifeult, Michel		No return.
	do	3162	Timec, Frederick	20 00	
	do	2880	Tribot, Edouard	20 00	
	do	2610	Coderre, Joseph		Services not proved.
	do	2605	Major *dit* Beautrain, St. Lue		Services not proved.
	do	2176	Marin, François		Services not proved.
	do	572	Marois, François		Services not proved.
	do	132	Primard, J. Jacques		Services not proved.
	do	3386	Latour, Joseph		On list for 1st July, 1877.
	do	396	St. Maurice, Justinien		Services not proved.
NAPIERVILLE	Napierville	594	Granger, Claude	20 00	
	do	261	Hebert, Michel	20 00	
	do	3064	Lemieux, Michel	20 00	
	do	596	Montminy, Jean	20 00	
	do	593	Morin, Laurent	20 00	
	do	597	Paré, Louis	20 00	
	do	99	Beaudoin, Etienne	20 00	
	Sherrington	941	Chaperon, Joseph	20 00	
	do	1206	Giroux, Pierre	20 00	
	do	3123	Patenaude, Pierre	20 00	

PENSIONS TO MILITIAMEN OF 1812-15.—Continued.

PROVINCE OF QUEBEC.—Continued.

Electoral District.	Post Office.	Number of Case.	Name of Militiaman.	Amount Paid.	Remarks.
				$ cts.	
NAPIERVILLE.— Continued	Sherrington	806	Pinsonnault, Paul	20 00	
	do	807	Poissant, Jacques	20 00	
	do	1632	Robert, François	20 00	
	St. Edmond	2591	Beaubrin, Gabriel	20 00	
	do	1680	Chaperon, Jean B	20 00	
	do	1688	Chenail, Antoine	20 00	
	do	1449	Deline, Antoine	20 00	
	do	1448	Lauctot, Alexis	20 00	
	do	2204	Richard, François	20 00	
	do	1757	Rougeau, Jean B	20 00	
	do	2481	Sorel, Jacques	20 00	
	St. Michel	1796	Boissonnault, François		Dead.
	do	1797	Gauthier, Antoine	20 00	
	do	2502	Hubert, Paul	20 00	
	do	1799	Menard, Pierre	20 00	
	do	2116	Pelletier, Clement	20 00	
	do	1795	Raymond, Jean B	20 00	
	do	2004	Ricard, Etienne	20 00	
	St. Remi	1886	Barrette, Louis	20 00	
	do	808	Briault, Louis	20 00	
	do	1809	Brisson, Joseph		Dead.
	do	1171	Brisson, Jean B	20 00	
	do	1165	Bouchard, Louis	20 00	
	do	2002	Dupuis, Constant	20 10	
	do	1166	Garand, Joseph		Dead.
	do	517	Oligny, Isaac	20 00	
	do	1172	Lacaille, Jean B	20 00	
	do	2636	Lefebvre, Jacques	00	
	do	1855	Lefebvre, Geoffroi	00	

PENSIONS TO MILITIAMEN OF 1812-15.—*Continued.*

PROVINCE OF QUEBEC.—*Continued.*

Electoral District.	Post Office.	Number of Case.	Name of Militiaman.	Amount Paid.	Remarks.
NAPIERVILLE.—				$ cts.	
Continued.	St. Rémi	1164	Letourneau, Pierre	20 00	
	do	2158	Patenaude, Charles	20 00	
	do	503	Poupard, Jean B	20 00	
NICOLET	Becancour	955	Dumont, Jean B	20 00	
	do	953	Lamontagne, F	20 00	
	do	952	Leblanc, Jacques	20 00	
	do	1768	Marceau, Germain	20 00	
	do	954	Montambeau, Michel	20 00	
	Gentilly	2015	Beaudet, Amable		Dead.
	do	231	Fortier, Thomas		Dead.
	do	298	Poisson, Joseph	20 00	
	Nicolet	1997	Beaubien, Louis	20 00	
	do	400	Provencher, Louis	20 00	
	do	399	Réné, François	20 00	
	St. Angele	948	Bourgeois, Joseph	20 00	
	St. Celestin	1442	Charest, Modeste	20 00	
	do	467	Gagnon, Ambroise	20 00	
	do	1441	Morin, Jean B	20 00	
	St. Gertrude	1544	Bourbeau, Joseph	20 00	
	St. Gregoire	296	Beliveau, Jean B	20 00	
	do	2633	Desrnisseau, Louis	20 00	
	do	693	Héon, Charles	20 00	
	do	260	Leblanc, Etienne	20 00	
	do	2289	Boisvert, Louis	20 00	
	St. Monique	1279	Duff, Charles	20 00	
	do	1203	Milot, Joseph	20 00	
	do	1440	Poirier, Pierre	20 00	
	St. Pierre les Becquets	1198	Brousseau, Isidore	20 00	
	do	1199	Brousseau, Martin		Dead.

PENSIONS TO MILITIAMEN OF 1812-15.—*Continued.*

PROVINCE OF QUEBEC.—*Continued.*

Electoral District.	Post Office.	Number of Case.	Name of Militiaman.	Amount Paid.	Remark.
				$ cts.	
NICOLETT.—*Con...*	St. Pierre les Becquets............	1197	Pepin, Olivier......	20 00	
	do ...	1200	Houle, Aiexis..............	20 00	
OTTAWA.........	Aylmer	3039	Martel, Louis	... .	Services not proved.
	do	3469	Leonard, François........	....	Services not proved.
	Buckingham	51	Maillé, Pierre	20 00	
	Eardley	1968	Cadieux, Antoir.:.	20 00	
	Hartwell	2597	Turpin, Eustacho	....	Dead.
	Hull	2917	Hurthubise, Pierre	20 00	
	do	1678	Lepage, Michel	20 00	
	do	2905	Lanctot, Antoine	20 00	
	do	1838	Ouellet, Paschal	20 00	
	do	2169	Parent, Joseph..............	....	No return.
	do ....,...	3220	Prejent, Louis	20 00	
	do	3215	Sabourin, François..	20 00	
	do	3452	Bessette, Etienne	....	On list for 1st July, 1877.
	Ange Gardien	3026	Belanger, Pierre............	20 00	
	Masham	3394	Ayotte, Charles............	....	Complete for 1st July, 1877.
	Montabello...........	2372	Cliche, J. B...............	....	Dead.
	do	3387	Lebeau, J. B.......	20 00	
	do	3311	Gauthier, Joseph..........	20 00	
	do	3253	Racicot, Charles............	20 00	
	do	3308	Lavoie, Jean B.............	....	Services not proved.
	Papineauville	3200	Céré, Gabriel	20 00	
	do	3127	Claude, André	20 00	
	do	3120	Daoust, Charles	20 00	
	do	2639	Dumanthet, Hippolyte....	20 00	
	do	3106	Gauthier, J. B.......... ..	20 00	
	do	2903	Hilman, Charles............	20 00	
	do	960	Lauzon, Joseph	20 00	

PENSIONS TO MILITIAMEN OF 1812-15 —Continued.

PROVINCE OF QUEBEC.—Continued.

Electoral District.	Post Office.	Number of case	Name of Militiaman.	Amount Paid.	Remarks.
				$ cts.	
OTTAWA.—Con	do	3130	Thiminenr, Toussaint ...	20 00	
	Ripon	1690	Laudriau, Jean M	20 00	
	do	1954	Quenville, Jean B	20 00	
	St. André Avellin.	1409	Guilmont, Joseph	20 00	
	do	2427	Leroux, Pierre..	20 00	
	Templeton (East)..	2907	Brunette, Janvier	20 00	
	do	1508	Laurin, François	20 00	
	do	393	Moreau, Jean B	20 00	
	do	2545	Robidoux, Pierre..	20 00	
	Thurso	5130	Forette, Charles	20 00	
	do	3366	Jereau, Antoine.		Services not proved.
	Wright	2870	Langlois, Urbain	20 00	
	do	31.8	Proulx, Hyacinthe		No Return.
	do	3044	Ethiér, Augustin		Services not proved.
	Wakefield	1676	Carman, William	20 00	
	Maniwaki	3300	Vanasse, François	20 00	
	do	3352	Winegonite, Antoine....	20 00	
	do	3353	Wanseinskete, Michel....		Services not proved.
PONTIAC	Allumettes	2146	McDonell, Alex. H	20 00	
	Calumet Island	2338	Giroux, Frs. X	20 00	
	Colfield	396	Smith, Walton		De id.
	Portage du Fort...	3274	Chartrain Gabriel	20 00	
PORTNEUF	Cap. Santé	27	Chaillé, Urbain	20 00	
	do	25	Falardeau, Joseph	20 00	
	do	89	Leclere, Joseph	20 00	
	Deschambault	994	Page, L. C		Dead
	Portneuf	26	Beauchemin, Jean B		Dead.
	PointauxTrembles	1249	Gravelle, Etienne	20 00	
	do	631	Grenier, Hyacinthe		Dead.
	do	2	Larue, Joseph F	20 00	

PENSIONS TO MILITIAMEN OF 1812-15.—*Continued.*

PROVINCE OF QUEBEC.— *Continued.*

Electoral District.	Post Office.	Number of Case.	Name of Militiaman.	Amount Paid.	Remarks.
				$ cts.	
PORTNEUF.--(*Con.*)	St. Augustin	29	Souiard, Jean	20 00	
	St. Basile	159	Duchemin, François	20 00	
	do	775	Filion, Olivier	20 00	
	do	346	Germain, Chrysologue	20 00	
	do	348	Piché, Adrien	20 00	
	St. Casimir	1537	Douville, Oilvier		Dead.
	do	946	Grinard, Jean B	20 00	
	do	626	L'Abbé, Ētienne	20 00	
	do	627	Therien, Pierre	20 00	
	do	1732	Thibault, Joseph	20 00	
	St. Raymond	630	Brosseau, Michel	20 00	
QUEBEC.	Ancienne Lorette	1974	Drolet, Jacques	20 00	
	do	1973	Gauvin, Louis		Dead.
	Beauport	295	Hinet, François		Dead.
	do	2383	Boulet, Charles	20 00	
	do	573	Côté, Ulric	20 00	
	do	1594	Gingras, Charles	20 00	
	do	980	Gingue, Jean	20 00	
	do	742	Giroux, F. X	20 00	
	do	2966	Parent, Michel		Dead.
	do	1979	Poulin, François	20 00	
	do	547	Gendron, Jean	20 00	
	Charlesbourg	2924	Harette, Ambroise	20 00	
	do	2273	Bédard, Stanislas		Dead.
	do	2276	Bourré, Louis	20 00	
	do	1978	Delage, Joseph	20 00	
	do	2805	Lafrance, Pierre	20 00	
	do	2957	Potvin, François	20 00	
	do	2274	Proteau, Jacques	20 00	

PENSIONS TO MILITIAMEN OF 1812-15.—*Continued.*

PROVINCE OF QUEBEC.—*Continued.*

Electoral District.	Post Office.	Number of Case.	Name of Militiaman.	Amount Paid.	Remarks.
				$ cts.	
QUEBEC.—(*Con.*)	Charlesbourg........	1976	Villeneuve, Joseph.......	20 00	
	do	508	Wyse, Frederick...........	20 00	
	do	3298	Bédard, Gabriel..........	20 00	
	Sillery Cove........	1916	Gignac, Jean Am........	20 00	
	St. Ambroise........	2119	Bédard, Gabriel..........	20 00	
	do	1995	Cardinal, Jean B.........	20 00	
	do	1743	Daigle, Jean J..	20 00	
	do	1992	Durand, Louis..............	20 00	
	do	2335	Lepire, Thomas............	20 00	
	do	1993	Pageau, Joan B............	15 00	
	do	1991	Pageau, François..........	....	Dead.
	do	1991	Verret, Jean B.	20 00	
	Queb c	575	Bertrand, François........	20 00	
	do	847	Bezeau, Joseph...........	20 00	
	do	420	Binet, Antoine	20 00	
	do	599	Boulianne, Thomas........	20 00	
	do	1870	Brière, Augustin.....	....	Dead.
	do	1217	Butler, Simon.....	20 00	
	do	792	Chartrain, Jacques........	20 00	
	do	1546	Cloutier, Joseph..........	20 00	
	do	2118	Cadoret, Charles..	20 00	
	do	1147	Dorer, Joseph.....	20 00	
	do	2827	Duré, Louis.......	20 00	
	do	739	Dorval, Jean B.............	20 00	
	do	744	Dusault, Jean B..........	20 00	
	do	1388	Delage, Joseph............	20 00	
	do	586	Fredet, François...........	....	Dead.
	do	420	Giroux, Jean........	20 00	
	do	569	Glackemeyer, Edouard..	20 00	

PROVINCE OF QUEBEC.—*Continued.*

Electoral District.	Post Office.	Number of Case.	Name of Militiaman	Amount Paid.	Remarks.
				$ cts.	
QUEBEC.—*Con.*	Quebec	2013	Gosselin, Nicholas	20 00	
	do	2920	Guilmette, Augustin	20 00	
	do	1742	Griffard, Etienne	20 00	
	do	166	Guerard, Jean	20 00	
	do	978	Gamache, Louis	20 00	
	do	1744	Bienveux, Charles	20 00	
	do	791	Huppé, Louis	20 00	
	do	2319	Jobin, Jean B	20 00	
	do	793	Lavoie, Joseph	20 00	
	do	209	Martin, Michel	20 00	
	do	1826	Moyen, François	20 00	
	do	2946	Plamondon, Philippe	20 00	
	do	695	Paquet, Pierre	20 00	
	do	183	Paquet, François	20 00	
	do	1507	Paquet, Pierre	20 00	
	do	875	Provencal, Jean		Dead.
	do	85	Renaud, F. X	20 00	
	do	602	Rhéaume, Joseph	20 00	
	do	2199	Richard, Paschal		Dead.
	do	2120	St Antoine, Charles	20 00	
	do	1243	St. Hilaire, Auguste	20 00	
	do	2334	Trudel, Louis	20 00	
	do	885	Terriault, Pierre C	20 00	
	do	681	Turgeon, Louis	20 00	
	do	427	Vallee, Charles	20 00	
	do	3761	Laforce, Joseph		Services not prove'.
	Sorel	685	Bussière, Joseph	20 00	
	do	2421	Cournoyer, Claude	20 00	
	do	2581	Cournoyer, Prisque		Dead.

PENSIONS TO MILITIAMEN OF 1812-15 —*Continued.*

PROVINCE OF QUEBEC.— *Continued.*

Electoral District.	Post Office.	Number of Case.	Name of Militiaman.	Amount Paid.	Remarks.
				$ cts.	
RICHELIEU.—*Con.*	Sorel	1530	Mainville, Jean B		No return.
	do	1354	Paul, Paschal L	20 00	
	do	698	Peltier, Jean B..	20 00	
	do	362	Plass, John Fred..	20 0.	
	do	691	Pontbriand, Jean	20 00	
	do	2252	Rochette, Michel	20 00	
	do	686	Crevier, Jean B	20 00	
	do	892	Ferrien, Benj		Dead.
	do	2583	Thibault, François	20 00	
	do	690	Gautara, Jean B	20 00	
	do	2353	Carrier, Joseph	20 00	
	do	652	Cournoyer, Joseph	20 00	
	do	654	Gauthier, Jean B	20 00	
	do	1391	Joly, Antoine		Dead.
	do	2551	Lagassé, Alexandre	20 00	
	do	681	Lamère, Pierre	20 00	
	do	2600	Lava ve, Pierre	20 00	
	do	199	Leith, Alexandre		Dead.
	do	3151	Vihandré, Barthelemi		Services not proved
	do	3376	Tutremble, Antoine		Services not proved.
	St. Anne	2514	Harpin, Andre	20 00	
	do	958	Turmer, Jerôme	20 0
	St. Marcel	151	Sorpadelaine, André	20 00	
	do	1619	Dalpe, Antoine	20 00	
	do	3095	Dessault, Joseph	20 00	
	do	1510	Gagnon, Jean B	20 00	
	do	1512	Robidou, Regis	20 00	
	St. Ours	2691	Allaire, Chrysologue	20 00	
	do	3144	Arseneau, Jean	20 00	

PENSIONS TO MILITIAMEN OF 1812-15.—*Continued*

PROVINCE OF QUEBEC.—*Continued.*

Electoral District.	Post Office.	Number of Case.	Name of Militiaman.	Amount Paid.	Remarks.
				$ cts.	
RICHELIEU.—*Con.*	St. Ours............	1938	Boivin, Paul..............	20 00	
	do	2362	Charbonneau, Pierre.....	....	Dead.
	do	2948	Faneuf, Louis............	20 00	
	do	1937	Godbout, Ambroise	20 00	
	do	1888	Fredette, Athanase.......	20 00	
	do	2586	Girouard, Louis...........	20 00	
	do	2053	Labossière, Jean B......	20 00	
	do	1939	Lelœuf, Julien..........	20 00	
	do	2944	St. Godard, Pierre........	20 00	
	St. Robert	2589	Leblanc, Basile............	20 00	
	St. Roch............	561	Beaudreau, Louis........	20 00	
	do	563	Chapdelaine, Antoine...	20 00	
	do	565	Hebert, Jean B...........	20 00	
	do	562	Pichette, François......	20 00	
	do	379	Rowse, Henry............	20 00	
	St. Victoire............	1327	Bordier, Joseph	20 00	
	do	1073	Dufault, Paul......	20 00	
	do	1071	Lavallé, Augustin	20 00	
	do	890	Lefort, Jean B.......	20 00	
	do	612	Millette, Claude............	20 00	
	do	1877	Mathieu, Joseph	20 00	
	do	603	Nelson, Alfred	20 00	
	do	1075	Desorcy, Alexis	20 00	
	do	1074	Dufault, Etienne	20 00	
	do	1072	Ethier, Jacques.	20 00	
	do	3115	Lavallé Pierre	20 00	
	do	687	Thibault, François.	20 00	
RICHMOND	Brompton Falls.....	2123	Houle, Charles......	....	No return.
	Danville.....	931	Emerson, Luthier	20 00	

S3

PENSIONS TO MILITIAMEN OF 1812-15.—*Continued.*

PROVINCE OF QUEBEC.—*Continued.*

Electoral District.	Post Office.	Number of Class.	Name of Militiaman.	Amount Paid.	Remarks.
				$ cts.	
RICHMOND.—*Con...*	Danville............	933	Morrill, Joseph...........	20 00	
	Richmond..........	2301	St. Cyr, Joseph..........	20 00	
	do	2958	Ledoux, Noel............	20 00	
	do	2579	Duperon, François.......	....	Services not proved.
	Stoke Centre.......	3091	Biron, Augusti.....	20 00	
RIMOUSKI............	Assomption de MeNider.	2177	Gendron, Prudent........	20 00	
	Matane............	250	Bernier, François........	20 00	
	Rimouski............	205	Lepage Honoré..........	20 00	
	St. Angèle..	374	Ouellet, Paul............	20 00	
	do	2832	Emond, Firmin.....	20 00	
	St. Cecile du Bic...	457	Collin, Joseph....	20 00	
	do ..	521	Gagnon, Firmin..........	20 00	
	St. Fabien..........	375	Gagné Denis.....	20 00	
	Ste. Luce............	1234	Faucher, Louis...........	20 00	
	de	1381	Lafrance, Charles........	20 00	
	do	1382	Mignault, Charles........	20 00	
	do	3290	Lavoie, Magloire..........	20 00	
	St. Moïse............	301	Morisset, Jean B.........	20 00	
	St. Octave de Metis	2781	Pelletier, Germain.......	20 00	
	St. Simon............	217	Lemieux, François........	20 00	
	do	216	Roy, Joseph.............	20 00	
	Tessierville........	2250	Collard, Thomas..........	20 00	
ROUVILLE	Abbottsford......	532	Caudal, Michel..........	20 00	
	do	566	Cote, Joseph..........	20 00	
	do	1015	Goddu, Joseph...........	20 00	
	Canrobert..........	1550	Brosleur, Basile..........	20 00	
	do	1553	Caron, Jean Frs..........	20 00	
	do	1556	Choquet, Jean B.........	20 00	
	do	1548	Desmarais, Pierre C......	20 00	

70.—6½

PENSIONS TO MILITIAMEN OF 1812-15.—*Continued.*

PROVINCE OF QUEBEC.—*Continued.*

Electoral District.	Post Office	Number of Case.	Name of Militiaman.	Amount Paid.	Remarks.
				$ cts	
ROUVILLE.—*Con...*	Canrobert	1554	Duclos, Louis...............	20 00	
	do	1552	Giboleau, Alexis..........	20 00	
	do	1549	Laporte, Joseph..........	20 00	
	do	1555	Sicard, Philibert.	....	Dead.
	do	1730	Raymond, André.	20 00	
	do	2442	Vaduais, Joseph............	20 00	
	do	2598	Catudal, Jean B............	20 00	
	do	2619	Loret, Joseph...............	20 00	
	do	2781	Poisson, Charles...........	20 00	
	Ste. Angele.	3090	Gaborian, Paschal........	20 00	
	do	2417	Tetrault, Victor..........	20 00	
	do	2892	Gervais, Pierre............	20 00	
	St. Césaire	1731	Bourbeau, Jean	20 00	
	do	221	Chanoine, Basile.........	20 00	
	do	1044	Dumas, Charles...........	20 00	
	do	222	Girard, François..	20 00	
	do	1041	Lagorce, Jean............	20 00	
	do	3047	Leblanc, Marc...........	20 00	
	do	224	Menard, Etienne...........	20 00	
	do	223	Pichette, Augustin........	20 00	
	do	1015	Vien, Charles..............	20 00	
	do	1219	Montplaisir, Guillaume..	20 00	
	St. Hilaire............	411	Côté, Toussaint...	20 00	
	do	442	Côté, Charles	20 00	
	do	413	Halde, Jean B	20 00	
	do	817	Lussier, Louis.....	20 00	
	St. Jean Baptiste...	1046	Brouillet Joseph	20 00	
	do ...	369	Chicoine, Victor...........	20 00	
	do ...	2453	Desautels, Michel..........	20 00	

PENSIONS TO MILITIAMEN OF 1812-15.—*Continued.*

PROVINCE OF QUEBEC.—*Continued.*

Electoral District.	Post Office	Number of Case.	Name of Militiaman.	Amount Paid.	Remarks.
				$ cts.	
ROUVILLE.—*Con...*	St. Jean Baptiste...	1966	Farrand, Charles..........	20 00	
	do ...	2485	Labonté, François X.....	20 00	
	do ...	1374	Lemonde, Michel..........	20 00	
	do ...	366	Lemonde, Joseph.	20 00	
	du ...	1106	Levêsque, François......	20 00	
	do ...	1377	Mainville, Pierre...........	....	Dead.
	do ...	444	Marcoux, Marcel	20 00	
	do ...	645	Meunier, François.........	....	Dead.
	do ...	2940	Patenaude, Ambr. se....	20 00	
	do ...	610	Tetreau, Dominique	20 00	
	do ...	3273	Mazurette, André.........	20 00	
	do ...	3346	Duclos, Gabriel...	....	Services not proved.
	Ste. Marie..........	368	Bedard, Jean B.............	20 00	
	do	367	Patenaude, Joseph	....	Services not proved.
	do	3138	Longtin, Pierre...........	20 00	
	do	3389	Parent, Louis	....	Services not proved.
	Village Richelieu..	3208	Barré, Jean B	20 00	
	do ...	3078	Bessette, Joseph C	20 00	
SHEFFORD..........	Ely	195	Milette, Jean B........	20 00	
	do	801	Stehène, Louis.....	20 00	
	Milton Corner	2646	Roger, François...........	20 00	
	Roxton Falls	172	Chevalt, Pierre	20 00	
	do	342	Demers, Pierre	20 00	
	Roxton Pond........	703	Stehène, Jean B............	20 00	
	do	2092	Daigneau, André...........	....	Services not proved.
	Shefford, West......	2524	Davis, William............	20 00	
	do	1299	Laurence, Durilla........	20 00	
	do	712	Mitchell, Archibald......	20 00	
	Stukeley, North....	2615	Côté, Gaspard	20 00	

80

PENSIONS TO MILITIAMEN OF 1812-15.—*Continued.*

PROVINCE OF QUEBEC.—*Continued.*

Electoral District.	Post Office.	Number of Case.	Name of Militiaman.	Amount Paid.	Remarks.
				$ cts.	
SHEFFORD.—*Con...*	Stukeley, North....	194	Gosselin, François........	20 00	
	do	1254	Jarret, Etienne...........	20 00	
	do	2178	Macfarlane, Malcolm.....	20 00	
	do	2181	Marcoux, Joseph.........	20 00	
	do	805	Payette, Jean...........	20 00	
	do	3142	Sevigny, Etienne........	20 00	
	do	323	Cinq-Mars, Etienne......	20 00	
	do	3295	Choquette, Antoine......	20 00	
	do	2593	Brissette, Joseph........	20 00	
	Waterloo	2182	Boucher, François........	20 00	
	do	1346	Clark, Daniel...........	20 00	
	do	2179	Kief, John.............	20 00	
	do	2180	Morisseau, Louis........	20 00	
	do	790	Rougier, Pierre..........	20 00	
SHERBROOKE........	Ascot Corner.......	2866	Cyr, Firmin		Service not proved.
	Lennoxville.........	541	Royer, François..........	20 00	
	Sherbrooke.........	2088	Carriere, Charles........	20 00	
	do	1999	Poirier, Joseph.........	20 00	
	do	3116	Phaneuf, François		On list for 1st July, 1877.
SOULANGES	Coteau Landing ...	2143	Merleau, Joseph.........	20 00	
	Coteau du Lac	2832	Boyer, François..........	20 00	
	do	2081	Clement, Pierre........	20 00	
	do	2143	Filion, Amédé...........	20 00	
	do	1536	Grenier, François	20 00	
	do	2595	Huneault, Joseph........	20 00	
	do	2868	Leclerc, Antoine	20 00	
	do	1306	Levac, François..........	20 00	
	do	3027	Sauvé, Joachim..........	20 00	
	do	2091	St. Denis, Joseph.	20 00	

PENSIONS TO MILITIAMEN OF 1812-15.—*Continued.*

PROVINCE OF QUEBEC.—*Continued.*

Electoral District.	Post Office.	Number of Case.	Name of Militiaman.	Amount Paid.	Remarks.
				$ cts.	
SOULANGES—*Con.* Coteau du Lac.....		3489	Gerard, Jean B.....	....	Services not proved.
	do	1533	Waquiere, Jean	....	Dead.
	do	3483	Bourbonnais, J. B.........	....	Services not proved.
	do	3263	Morneau, Antoine........	20 00	
	Les Cedres..........	1461	Coutlée, Théotime........	20 00	
	do	667	Lalonde, Jean B.....	20 00	
	do	668	Veronneau, Joseph	20 00	
	Mount Joy	127	McCuaig. John B........	20 00	
	Pont Chateau.......	3345	Daudurand, Jean B......	20 00	
	do	3458	Deschamps, Jean B...	....	On list for 1st July, 1877.
	do	3463	Lanouette, Godefroy.....	....	Services not proved.
	Rivière Beaudet....	3251	Challe, Louis	20 00	
	do	3252	Fournier, Jacques........	20 00	
	do	3260	Sauvé, Jean B.	20 00	
	do	3261	Sauvé, Alexis.....	20 00	
	do	2343	McKee, William............	20 00	
	do	3302	Leblanc, Etienne..	20 00	
	St. Clet..............	1301	Consineau, Luc	20 00	
	do	62	Garand, Jean.............	20 00	
	St. Polycarpe........	3299	Bray, Pierre.....	20 00	
	do	318	Asselin, Albert............	20 00	
	do	320	Asselin, Augustin........	20 00	
	do	324	Biron, Gregoire	20 00	
	do	1303	Bray, François.....	20 00	
	do	2035	Daoust, Jean B............	20 00	
	do	323	Desjardins, Louis..........	20 00	
	do	3315	Lalonde, Joseph	20 00	
	do	319	Glande, Nicholas..........	....	Dead.
	do	317	Sauvé, Jean B.............	20 00	
	do	322	Vendette, Jacques........	20 00	

PENSIONS TO MILITIAMEN OF 1812-15.—*Continued.*

PROVINCE OF QUEBEC.—*Continued.*

Electoral District.	Post Office	Number of Case.	Name of Militiaman.	Amount Paid.	Remarks.
				$ cts.	
SOULAGENS—*Con.*	St. Polycarpe.......	3238	Dubeau, Jean B...........	20 00	
	do	3291	Houle, Martin...	20 00	
	do	3303	Bissonnette, Paul.........	20 00	
	do	3330	Avon, François............	....	Services not proved.
	St. Zotique........ .	270	Bissonnette, Joachim.....	20 00	
	do	2658	Lalonde, Dominique......	20 00	
	do	268	Lalonde, Jean D...........	20 00	
	do	269	Lalonde, Joseph...........	20 00	
	do	2632	Sauré, Louis..............	20 00	
	do	3233	Montpetit, Augustin......	20 00	
	do	3254	Lalonde-Geneva, Joseph	20 00	
	do	3300	Cholette, Hyacinthe......	20 00	
	do	3314	Cedilot, Gabriel...........	....	Services not proved.
	do	3317	Greffe, Guillaume.........	....	Services not proved.
	do	3319	Provost, Bénoni.......	....	Services not proved.
STANSTEAD...........	Ayer's Flatts........	3364	Ilich, Joseph...........	20 00	
	do	838	Oliver, William...........	20 00	
	Barnston	629	Burroughs, William......	20 00	
	Hatley................	2585	Desance, Charles	20 00	
	Magog.............	2563	Keet, David............	20 00	
	do	2564	Wheeler, Jacob...........	20 00	
	St. Hermenigilde...	2623	Hebert, Isaac.	20 00	
	South Barnston.....	1358	Burroughs, Joseph........	20 00	
ST. HYACINTHE. ..	La Presentation....	641	Leblanc, Jean D..........	20 00	
	St. Barnabé.	901	Archambault, O...........	20 00	
	St. Charles..	900	Caron, Pierre......	20 00	
	do	2898	Brodeur, Jean B............	20 00	
	do	2901	Gauthier, François........	20 00	
	do	2900	Tetreau, Amable......	20 00	
	St. Damase...........	359	Archambault, H	....	Dead.

PENSIONS TO MILITIAMEN OF 1812-15.—*Continued.*

PROVINCE OF QUEBEC.—*Continued.*

Electoral District.	Post Office	Number of Case.	Name of Militiaman.	Amount Paid.	Remarks.
				$ cts.	
ST. HYACINTHE—(*Continued.*)........	St. Damase..	560	Coyteux, Joseph...........	20 00	
	do	549	Piché, Joseph.............	20 00	
	do	3247	Vachon, François..........	20 00	
	St. Denis	3134	Brien, Joseph.............	20 00	
	do	1392	Beaulieu, Louis........ ...	20 00	
	do	1290	Bonin, Pierre............ ..	20 00	
	do	1293	Bonin, Gabriel.............	20 00	
	do	1291	Dillaire, Guillaume.....	20 00	
	do	1963	Dragon, André	20 00	
	do	1905	Faneuf, François........	20 00	
	do	3326	Faneuf, Moïse	20 00	
	do	1289	Guertin, Louis....	20 00	
	do	1904	Guertin, Michel	20 00	
	do	2967	Merciér, Joseph	20 00	
	do	1294	Plante, Jean B............	....	Dead.
	do	1288	St. Pierre, Augustin.....	20 00	
	St. Hyacinthe.......	2087	Pion, Jean B..............	20 00	
	do	287	Basinct, Joseph....	20 00	
	do	1.9	Blanchette, Charles	20 00	
	do	610	Bonaquet, Charles.........	20 00	
	do	3111	Carpentier, Isidore.......	20 00	
	do	800	Civallér, Claude..	20 00	
	do	2 74	Clopin, Jean B	20 00	
	do	1935	Chagnon, Joseph	20 00	
	do ...	1942	Desmarteau, B. Pierre...	20 00	
	do	1396	Diamault, Paul...........	20 00	
	do	858	Langelier, Jean B	20 00	
	do	725	Lecours, Charles...... ...	....	No return.
	do	3050	Meunier, François........	20 00	

PENSIONS TO MILITIAMEN OF 1812-15.—*Continued.*

PROVINCE OF QUEBEC.—*Continued.*

Electoral District.	Post Office.	Number of Case.	Name of Militiaman.	Amount Paid.	Remarks.
				$ cts.	
ST. HYACINTHE— (*Continued.*)	St. Hyacinthe	2650	Perreault, Louis	20 00	
	do	288	Pin, Joseph	20 00	
	do	286	Query, Louis	20 00	
	do	857	Robitaille, Joseph	20 00	
	do	2123	Roy. Jreques	20 00	
	do	401	Sasseville, François	20 00	
	do	32:8	Franchere, Léandre	20 00	
	St. Jude	359	Cloutier, Prospere	20 00	
	do	2230	Dauphinais, Louis	20 00	
	do	1132	Delorme, Antoine		Dead.
	do	2279	Dumas, Nicholas	20 00	
	do	285	Gervais, Michel	20 00	
	do	1070	Girouard, Pierre	20 00	
	do	1583	Lafrenalè, Athanase	20 00	
	do	289	Mailloux, François	20 00	
	do	8331	Chaput, Louis		Services not proved.
St. JOHNS	Grande Ligne	3137	Seneeal, Jean B		Dead.
	Lacadie	2884	Roulier, Joseph	20 00	
	do	3036	Richard, Réné	20 00	
	do	2857	Morin, Paul	20 00	
	Lacolle	2071	Barrière, Denis	20 00	
	do	1798	Bonhomme, Jacques	20 00	
	do	1517	Carpentier, Laurent	20 00	
	do	1570	Duquet, Etienne	20 00	
	do	1516	Gauthier, Joseph	20 00	
	do	2712	Labonté, François	20 00	
	do	1968	Larau, Pierre	20 00	
	do	1314	Menard, Alexis	20 00	
	do	1515	Pagé, Jean B	20 00	

PENSIONS TO MILITIAMEN OF 1812-15.—*Continued.*

PROVINCE OF QUEBEC.—*Continued.*

Electoral District.	Post Office.	Number of Case.	Name of Militiaman.	Amount Paid.	Remarks.
				$ cts.	
ST. JOHNS.- Con...	Lacolle......	1513	Scriver, William...........	20 00	
	do	3381	Dateau, François.......	....	Services not proved.
	St. Johns......	2918	Bonin, Joseph	20 00	
	do	2020	Caillé Joseph.	....	Left limits.
	do	2964	Cartier, Pierre	20 00	
	do	2069	Daigneau, Michel............	....	Dead.
	do	2007	Emond, Christophe...	....	Dead.
	do	2963	Hubert, Antoine.............	....	Left limits.
	do	2065	Lacoste, Pierre	20 00	
	do	2963	Monbleau, André...	20 00	
	do	2805	Montreuil, Jacques........	....	Left limits.
	do	2962	Nadeau, Alexandre........	20 00	
	do	2063	Zoman, Gabriel	20 00	
	do	3035	Trahan, Dominique..	20 00	
	do	2066	Vincelette, Joseph	20 00	
	do	3338	Gervais, Pierre	20 00	
	St. Luc..............	2070	Maine, Jean B	20 00	
	. Valentin	733	Boissonnault, Nicholas...	20 00	
	do	728	Desjadon, Charles........	20 00	
	do	277	Demers, Nicholas	20 00	
	do	67	Hart, Frederick...........	20 00	
	do	1061	Trottier, Antoine..........	20 00	
	do	3232	Gendron, Vital	20 00	
	do	3263	Cloutier, Prisque..........	20 00	
	Stottsville............	3412	Lamoureux, David	....	On list for 1st July, 1877.
ST. MAURICE.......	Pointe du Lac	1901	Decoteau, Augustin......	20 00	
	do	180	Duplesis, Louis.............	20 00	
	do	2144	Dupont, Louis.............	20 00	
	do	1958	Gareau, Louis.......	20 00	

92

PENSIONS TO MILITIAMEN OF 1812-15.---*Continued.*

PROVINCE OF QUEBEC.—*Continued.*

Electoral District.	Post Office.	Number of age.	Name of Militiaman.	Amount Paid.	Remarks.
				$ cts.	
ST. MAURICE-*Con.*	Pointe du Lac ...	1793	Houle, Joseph	20 00	
	do	1080	Maheu, Alexis	20 00	
	Shawenegan	2649	Grenier, Alexis		Dead.
	St. Barnabé	2033	Bellemare, Augustin	20 00	
	do	1622	Boisvert, François	20 00	
	do	1081	Gelinas, Pierre	20 00	
	do	1621	Lacombe, Joachim	20 00	
	do	937	Melançon, Simon	20 00	
	St. Elie	1857	Vanasse, Charles	20 00	
	St. Etienne	3033	Bicard, David	20 00	
	St Sévère	263	Lamprond, Louis	20 00	
	do	264	Lamprond, Joseph	20 00	
	do	1357	LeBlanc, Jean	20 00	
	Vieilles Forges	1957	Loisvert, Jean B	20 00	
	do	2976	Landry, Jean B	20 00	
	Yamachiche	2205	Boisvert, Augustin		Dead.
	do	174	Hudon, Louis P	20 00	
	do	1498	Freny, Lesieur T	20 00	
	do	938	Pellerin, Paul	20 00	
	do	173	Robidas, François	20 00	
	do	3257	Feron, Jean	20 00	
THREE RIVERS...	Three Rivers	2098	Brunet, Joseph		Dead.
	do	109	Cadoret, Pierre	20 00	
	do	3093	Carrière, Louis		Dead.
	do	2790	Dufresne, Antoine	20 00	
	do	2002	Lacerte, Pierre	20 00	
	do	1324	Langlois, Joseph	20 00	
	do	1907	Martin, Olivier	20 00	
	do	2421	Massicotte, Jean B	20 00	

93

PENSIONS TO MILITIAMEN OF 1812-15.—*Continued.*.

PROVINCE OF QUEBEC.—*Continued.*

Electoral District.	Post Office.	Number of Case.	Name of Militiaman.	Amount Paid.	Remarks.
				$ cts.	
THREE RIVERS.— (Continued)......	Three Rivers............	2987	Muller, Charles	20 00	
	do	1214	Quessy, Joseph	20 00	
	do	2378	Robert, Etienne............	20 00	
	do	2989	Robichon, André.........	20 00	
	do	3270	Arel, Joachim............	20 00	
TERREBONNE	Ste. Adèle.....	385	Berthelette, Louis	20 00	
	do	386	Brousseau, Michel........	20 00	
	do	383	Forget, Pierre	20 00	
	do	388	Imbault, Jean B............	20 00	
	do	381	Latleur, Joachim...........	20 00	
	do	389	Longpré, Jérôme...........	20 00	
	do	390	Pilon, Louis	....	Dead.
	do	2933	Robert, Louis............	20 00	
	do	382	Lauzon, Joseph............	....	Services not proved.
	Ste. Agathe	380	Jeannotte, Basile	20 00	
	do	384	Sausé, François............	20 00	
	Ste. Anne des Plaines...............	709	Delisle, Etienne............	20 00	
	do ...	711	Derouin, Joseph............	20 00	
	do ...	710	Hogue, Dominique.........	20 00	
	St. Janvier	510	Limoges, Charles.........	20 00	
	do	509	Pâquet, Paul	20 00	
	do	511	Roture, Antoine	20 00	
	St. Jérome...........	1630	Alary, Louis......	20 00	
	do	1638	Alary, Jean M	20 00	
	do	835	Dorval, Ignace	20 00	
	do	832	Graton, Louis...............	20 00	
	do	834	Guenette, Jean	20 00	
	do	833	Renaud, Charles............	20 00	

PENSIONS TO MILITIAMEN OF 1812-15—*Continued.*

PROVINCE OF ONTARIO.—*Continued.*

Electoral District.	Post Office.	Number of Case.	Name of Militiaman.	Amount Paid.	Remarks.
				$ cts.	
TERREBONNE.— (*Continued*)......	St. Jérome	1697	Thibault. Jean.B......	20 00	
	do	1690	Villette, Augustin.........	20 00	
	do	1629	Bertrand, Jean B........	20 00	
	Ste. Marguerite....	1359	Charette, Charles........	20 00	
	do	387	Gladu, André.............	20 00	
	St. Sauveur...... ...	266	Provost, Pierre............	20 00	
	do	265	Tassé, Philibert...........	20 00	
	do	530	Tougas, Joseph...........	....	Dead.
	do	1602	Levellé, Joseph..........	20 00	
	uo	2125	Daragon, Jean B........	20 00	
	Ste. Thérese........	714	Regimbal, Pierre........	20 00	
	do	715	Jumenville, Michel......	20 00	
	do	713	Labelle, Toussaint.......	20 00	
	do	716	Pâquet, François..........	20 00	
	do	719	Chartrain, Joseph	....	No return.
TEMISCOUATA......	Cacouna.............	1231	Pelletier, Abraham......	20 00	
	Isle Verte..........	1235	Côté, Raphael.............	....	Dead.
	do	2282	Paré, Augustin	20 00	
	do	1230	Ouellet, François..	20 00	
	do	2261	Dionne, Pierre............	20 00	
	Notre Dame du Portage	1227	Laforest, François........	20 00	
	Rivière du Loup...	1226	Chamberland, Jean B....	20 00	
	Trois Pistoles.	895	Leclere, Alexis	....	Dead.
	St. Antonin	1229	Caouette, Joseph.........	....	Dead.
	St. Arsene	1233	Marchand, François. ...	20 00	
	St. Epiphane...	567	L'Italien, Joseph	20 00	
	St. Modeste...........	1233	Chamberland, François..	20 00	
	St. Paul de la Croix	1238	Leduc, Firmin	....	No return.

PENSIONS TO MILITIAMEN OF 1812-15.—*Continued.*

PROVINCE OF QUEBEC.—*Continued.*

Electoral District.	Post Office.	Number of Case.	Name of Militiaman.	Amount Paid.	Remarks.
				$ cts.	
TWO MOUNTAINS.	Oka	3100	Kenentoton, Ignace	20 00	
	do	3100	Onaquat-Kawa, Joseph.	20 00	
	do	3319	Mikons, Simon	20 00	
	do	3050	Annaietta, Simon		Services not proved.
	do	3348	Kapeyu, Vincent		Services not proved.
	St. Augustin	2553	Desjardins, Joseph	20 00	
	do	1665	Duquette, François	20 00	
	do	2554	Labelle, Jean M	20 00	
	do	2561	Leonard, Paul	20 00	
	do	2562	Ouellet, Alexis	20 00	
	do	2557	Ouellet, Jean B	20 00	
	do	2559	Tassé, Charles	20 00	
	do	2556	Verdon, Basile	20 00	
	do	2555	Denèche *dit* Luvictoire, Pierre		Services not proved.
	St. Benoit	203	Labouté, Jean D	20 00	
	do	2856	Laviolette, Jean B		Services not proved.
	St. Canut	378	Joly, Louis	20 00	
	St. Columban	377	Ouellet, Gabriel	20 00	
	St. Eustache	1692	Beauchamp, Joseph	20 00	
	do	3596	Belanger, Jean B	20 00	
	do	3016	Demers, Jean B	20 00	
	do	1694	Gironard, Luc	20 00	
	do	1693	Latour, Jerôme	20 00	
	do	786	Proulx, Jean B	20 00	
	do	1695	Savard, Jean B	20 00	
	do	1787	Miller, Jean	20 00	
	St. Hermas	1125	Doré, Jacques	20 00	
	do	3083	McKercher, John	20 00	

PENSIONS TO MILITIAMEN OF 1812-15.—*Continued.*

PROVINCE OF QUEBEC.—*Continued.*

Electoral District.	Post Office.	Number of Case.	Name of Militiaman.	Amount Paid.	Remarks.
				$ cts.	
TWO MOUNTAINS. (*Continued*).......	St. Hermas.............	1455	Pagé, Jean B........	26 00	
	do	1126	Pagé, François............	20 00	
	do	1124	Richer, Basile.............	20 00	
	do	1127	Sauvé, Luc	20 00	
	St. Joseph du Lac..	2548	Labelle, Joseph	20 00	
	do ..	2547	Lorain, Jean B	....	Dead.
	St. Monique	1661	Duquette, Joachin........	20 00	
	St. Placide	2438	Sauvé, Joseph............	20 00	
	St. Scholastique....	1607	Benoit, Frs. X.............	20 00	
	do	954	Fortier, Leonard.........	20 00	
	do	190	Gauthier, Joseph..	20 00	
	do	1465	Legault, Joseph...........	20 00	
	do	3341	Taillefer, Joseph	20 00	
	do	2518	Touchette, Charles........	20 00	
	do	307	Vermette, Joseph.........	20 00	
	do	1646	Lavigue, Arthur	20 00	
VAUDREUIL..........	Como.............	2307	Berlinquette, Joseph.....	20 00	
	do	1929	Hurthubise, Nicholas.....	20 00	
	do	1928	Lacombe, Jean B	20 00	
	Isle Perrot............	2213	Dubrule, Michel	20 00	
	do	2046	Dubreuil, Antoine........	20 00	
	do	735	Montpetit, Pierre........	20 00	
	do	736	Poirier, Michel............	20 00	
	Rigaud	2404	Bedard, Joseph	20 00	
	do	2403	Dumouchel, Ignace..	20 00	
	do	3107	Laframboise, Hubert......	20 00	
	do	2614	Lalonde, Joseph............	22 00	
	do	3117	Lefebvre, Joseph..........	20 00	
	do	3108	Mallet, Hyacinthe........	20 00	

PENSIONS TO MILITIAMEN OF 1812-15.—*Continued.*

PROVINCE OF QUEBEC.—*Continued.*

Electoral District.	Post Office.	Number of Case.	Name of Militiaman.	Amount Paid.	Remarks.
				$ cts.	
VAUDREUIL—*Con.*	Rigaud..	2533	Mallet, Theodore.	20 00	
	do	2552	Larocque, Louis	20 00	
	do	2541	Sabourin, François	20 00	
	do	2401	Seguin, François	20 00	
	do	2551	Seguin, Antoine	20 00	
	do	3327	Cardinal Dominique	20 00	
	do	2402	Vallée, Pierre	20 00	
	St. Justine	2542	Decœur, Louis	20 00	
	do	1305	Legault, Jean B	20 00	
	do	1302	Seguin, Joachim	20 00	
	do	2197	St. Amant, André	20 00	
	St. Marthe	2540	Bedard, Joachim	20 00	
	do	2543	Couturier, Hubert	20 00	
	do	3272	Deschamps, Joseph	20 00	
	Vaudreuil	2256	Cadieux, Jacques	20 00	
	do	459	Gamelin, Benjamin	20 00	
	do	1681	Gastonguay, Elie	20 00	
	do	1686	Lajoie, Joseph		Dead.
	do	1683	Larocque, Hyacinthe	20 00	
	do	2534	Lecuyer, Joseph	20 00	
	do	2045	Leger, Charles		Dead.
	do	1685	Poirier, Augustin	20 00	
	do	193	Martel, François	20 00	
	do	2308	Rose, François	20 00	
	do	1684	Sagala, Pierre	20 00	
	do	1930	Lecompte, Gabriel	20 00	
	do	2795	Therien, Jean B		Services not proved.

PENSIONS TO MILITIAMEN OF 1812-15 —*Continued.*

PROVINCE OF QUEBEC.--*Continued.*

Electoral District.	Post Office	Number of Case.	Name of Militiaman.	Amount Paid.	Remarks.
				$ cts.	
VERCHÈRES	Beloil	1055	Fournier, Alexis...........	20 00	
	do	1057	Hubert, Antoine...........	20 00	
	do	1770	Phaneuf, Hyacinthe......	20 00	
	do	1056	Pigeon, Augustin	20 00	
	Contrecœur.	1210	Allard, Paul...............	20 00	
	do	83	Dubois, Joseph..	20 00	
	do	417	Fournier, Joseph...........	20 00	
	do	418	Grenon, Joseph...........	20 00	
	do	416	Peltier, André............	20 00	
	do	30	Richard, Jérôme...........	20 00	
	do	419	Roy, Pierre...............	20 00	
	do	421	St. Onge, Antoine.......	20 00	
	St. Antoine	746	Archambault, Antoine..	20 00	
	do	749	Bourgeois, François......	20 00	
	do	1501	Cabana, Michel...........	20 00	
	do	747	Chevali, Joseph...........	20 00	
	do	715	Gaudette, François.......	....	Dead.
	do	718	Girouard, François.......	20 00	
	do	750	Gosselin, François.......	20 00	
	do	751	Roy, Amable	20 00	
	Ste. Julie...........	1218	Bardona, James...........	20 00	
	do	357	Charbonneau, Louis.....	20 00	
	do	358	Mongeau, Joseph...........	20 00	
	do	822	McDoff, Charles...........	20 00	
	St. Marc	635	Blanchard, Jean B	20 00	
	do	1605	Blanchard, Etienne......	20 00	
	do	632	Jeannotte, Joseph........	20 00	
	do	633	Fontaine, François	20 00	
	do	634	Legros, Michel	20 00	

PENSIONS TO MILITIAMEN OF 1812-15.—*Continued.*

PROVINCE OF QUEBEC.—*Continued.*

Electoral District.	Post Office.	Number of Case.	Name of Militiaman.	Amount Paid.	Remarks.
				$ cts.	
VERCHERES—*Con.*	St. Marc	2005	Robert, Joseph	20 00	
	Varennes	1749	Anbertin, Jean B	20 00	
	do	1753	Ayet, Joseph	20 00	
	do	1752	Dalpé, Hypolite	20 00	
	do	1751	Dalpé, Joseph	20 00	
	do	1754	Decelles, Antoine	20 00	
	do	1750	Lozeau, Jean B		Dead.
	do	1777	Neneeal, Louis	20 00	
	Verchères	75	Dachaud, François	20 00	
	do	1674	" Augustin	20 00	
	do	186	" ph	20 00	
	do	440	"	20 00	
	do	413	"	20 00	
	do	1216	Lucier,	20 00	
WOLFE	Ham, North	2026	Boulet, François	20 00	
	St Albert	2578	Gagné, Mathias	20 00	
	St. Camille	763	Beauchemin, Antoine	20 00	
	Wotton	251	Boisvert, Michel	20 00	
	do	762	Royer. Barthélemi	20 00	
	do	762	Cyr, Joseph	20 00	
	do	761	Gnouette, Louis		Dead.
	do	1596	Gosselin, Joachim		Dead
YAMASKA.	La Baie.	1268	Boisvert, Joseph	20 00	
	do	1824	Bournssn, Charles	20 00	
	do	425	Ganthier. Louis	20 50	
	do	422	Houle, Joseph	20 00	
	do	424	Maneeau, Charles	20 00	
	Rivière David	1415	Danis, Joseph	20 00	
	do	1922	Gnugin, Basile	20 00	

PENSIONS TO MILITIAMEN OF 1812-15.—Continued.

PROVINCE OF QUEBEC.—Continued.

Electoral District.	Post Office.	Number of Case.	Name of Militiaman.	Amount Paid.	Remarks.
				$ cts	
YAMASKA.—Con....	Rivière David........	1246	Langlois, Pierre............	20 00	
	do	606	Larivière, M...............	20 00	
	do	1281	Mondore, Jean...........	20 00	
	do	2537	Letendre, Jean D...........	20 00	
	do	3439	Pepin, Louis............	....	Services not proved.
	St. François du Lac	2425	Alarie, Charles..........	20 00	
	do	2237	Cartier, Augustin........	20 00	
	do	2238	Cartier, Jean..............	....	Dead.
	do	984	Chapdelaine, Joseph......	20 00	
	do	985	Caya, Louis...............	20 00	
	do	2235	Courchene, Jean B........	20 00	
	do	2988	Duguay, Joseph...........	20 00	
	do	986	Joyal, Antoine...........	20 00	
	do	1932	Martel, François..........	20 00	
	do	223	Nadeau, Alexis............	20 00	
	St. Michel............	121	Aulotte Joseph...........	....	Dead.
	do	606	Girard, Louis...........	20 00	
	do	1735	Parent, Louis	20 00	
	do	1736	Salvas, Joseph..	....	Dead.
	St. Pie de Guire....	2862	Cartier, Joseph.........	20 20	
	do ...	1247	Proulx, Pierre...........	20 00	
	St. Thomas.........	251	Allie, François..	20 00	
	do	252	Barbeau, Charles..........	20 00	
	do	665	Gagnon, François........	20 00	
	do	256	Hamel, Pierre...........	20 00	
	do	255	Joyal, Michel.............	20 00	
	do	3190	Annance, Simon	20 00	
	do	213	Bernier, Joseph...........	20 00	
	do	664	Côté, Jean B.............	20 00	

PENSIONS TO MILITIAMEN OF 1812-15.—*Con... ..d.*

PROVINCE OF QUEBEC.—*Concluded.*

Electoral District.	Post Office.	Number of Case.	Name of Militiaman.	Amount Paid.	Remarks.
				$ cts.	
YAMASKA.—*Con.*,...	St. Thomas...........	3139	Obumsawin, François....	20 00	
	St. Zephlrin.........	258	Morissette, Jean B	20 00	
	do	257	Rousseau, François	20 00	

PENSIONS TO MILITIAMEN OF 1812-15.—*Continued.*

PROVINCE OF NEW BRUNSWICK.

Electoral District.	Post Office.	Number of Case.	Name of Militiaman.	Amount Paid.	Remarks.
				$ cts.	
CHARLOTTE	Oak Bay	2241	Eastman, David		Services not proved.
	do	5280	Rideout, Benjamin		Services not proved.
	St. Andrews	2876	Boyd, James	20 00	
	do	3036	Stinson, James	20 00	
	St. Stephen	3496	Grant, William		Services not proved.
GLOUCESTER	Bathurst	3068	Degrace, Raphael	20 00	
	do	3103	Poirier, Hubert	20 00	
	Madisco	3062	Arseneau, Pierre	20 00	
	do	3061	Boudreau. Sebastien	20 00	
	Caraquet	3231	Cormier, Ambroise	20 00	
	do	3230	Lanteigne, Eloi	20 00	
	do	3229	Poirier, Carolus	20 00	
	Tracadie	3385	Vieneau, Athanase	20 00	
KENT	Buctouche	2760	Bastarache, Thadeus	20 00	
	do	2761	Casey, Beloni	20 00	
	do	2759	St. oie, Beloni	20 00	
	Cocagne	1903	Dupré, Honoré	20 00	
	do	1901	Guegen, Cyrille	20 00	
	do	1904	Guegen, Placide	20 00	
	do	1902	Lirette, Hubert	20 00	
	Kingston	2214	Fitzgerald, William		Dead.
	Richibucto	3089	McCully, Wm. Cochrane	20 00	
	do	2923	Richard, Damase	20 00	
	do	2924	Richard, Laurent		Dead.
	St. Louis	2928	Vautour, Romain	20 00	
KINGS	Studholm	3255	Chapman, Stephen C	20 00	
MADAWASKA	Edmonston	1740	Mingue (dit Lagacé), Dominique	20 00	
	St. Hilaire	2205	Michaud, Romain		Dead.
	St. Leonard	2306	Michaud, Laurent		Dead.

PENSIONS TO MILITIAMEN OF 1812-15.—*Continued.*

PROVINCE OF NEW BRUNSWICK.—*Concluded.*

Electoral District.	Post Office.	Number of Case.	Name of Militiaman.	Amount Paid.	Remarks.
				$ cts.	
WESTMORELAND..	Dalhousie	3149	Lapointe, Jean B.	20 00	
	Dorchester	3223	Palmer, John	20 00	
	do	2829	Legerre, Pierre		No return.
	Sackville	3243	Wry, George	20 00	'
	do	3415	Finesty, Winchworth		Services not proved.
	Tidish, West	2941	Leger, Fidele	20 00	
	Westmoreland	3236	Chapman, Joseph	20 00	
YORK	Fredericton	2864	Chassé, Firmin	20 00	
St JOHN	St. John	3222	Ross, John	20 00	

PENSIONS TO MILITIAMEN OF 1812-15.—*Continued.*

PROVINCE OF NOVA SCOTIA.

Electoral District.	Post Office.	Number of Case.	Name of Militiaman.	Amount Paid.	Remarks.
				$ cts.	
ANNAPOLIS	Annapolis	3176	Anderson, William		Services not proved.
	do	3306	Ruggles, T. W		do
	Clements Port	3491	Potter, John		do
	do	3493	Balcomb, James		do
	Granville	3500	Hall, Henry		do
	do	3504	Roach, Frederick		do
	do	3184	Starret, Jacob T		In abeyance
CUMBERLAND	Fox Harbour	2878	Munro, John	20 00	
	Gulf Shore	3216	McIvor, John	20 00	
	Pugwash River	3225	McPherson, Ewan	20 00	
	do	2863	Pace, Edmond		Services not proved.
	Wallace	2844	Dotten, James	20 00	
	do	2857	Fardiner, Knapp	20 00	
	do	3314	Fulton, William	20 00	
	do	2843	Huestis, James H	20 00	
	do	3001	McKenzie, John	20 00	
	do	3081	McFarlane, John	20 00	
	do	3068	McIver, John	20 00	
	do	3088	McNab, Welwood	20 00	
	do	3101	Ross, Donald	20 00	
	do	3098	Stewart, George	20 00	
	do	3066	Waugh, Welwood	20 00	
	do	3304	McNeil, Neil		do
	do	3305	Fontaine, James		do
	do	3306	Angevine, Peter		do
	do	3129	Smith, Abuor		do
COLCHESTER	Tatamagouche	3204	Tatric, George		do
	do	3237	McPherson, Neil		do
	do	3558	Matatalle, Lewis		do

PENSIONS TO MILITIAMEN OF 1812-15.—*Continued.*

PROVINCE OF NOVA SCOTIA.—*Continued.*

Electoral District.	Post Office.	Number of Case.	Name of Militiaman.	Amount Paid.	Remarks.
				$ cts.	
COLCHESTER — (*Continued*)	Tatamagouche	3350	Waugh, Samuel		Services not proved.
	do	3360	Patriquin, John		do
	Truro	3432	Cameron, Hugh		do
DIGBY	Bear River	3413	McDormand, Joel		do
	do	3494	Boggart, Samuel		do
	do	3426	Rice, John		do
	do	3492	Chute, James		do
	do	3462	Copeland, John		do
	Centreville	3384	Ramsay, Malcolm		do
	Digby	3475	Wade, James		do
	do	3477	Budd, Charles		do
	do	3478	Budd, James		do
	do	3479	Burnham, William		do
	do	3480	Litteney, John		do
	do	3481	Litteney, Thomas		do
	do	3482	Zeigler, William		do
	do	3483	Spur, Abraham		do
	do	3485	Hawksworth, A. E.		do
	Sandy Cove	3494	Carty, Silas		do
	Smith Cove	3497	Pratt, James W.		do
	do	3456	Cossette, Lewis		do
HANTS	do	3472	Suli, Daniel		do
	Brooklyn	3468	Lockhart, John		do
	Burlington	3509	Burgess, Noah		do
	Falmouth	3446	Potter, George		do
	Five Mills River	3438	Ettinger, Daniel		do
	Hantsport	3441	Crowell, William		do
	do	3442	Dickie, Samuel		do
	do	3443	Earle, John		do
	Newport	3432	Harvey, Archibald		do

76—8

PENSIONS TO MILITIAMEN OF 1812-15.—*Continued.*

PROVINCE OF NOVA SCOTIA.—*Concludued.*

Electoral District	Post Office.	Number of Case.	Name of Militiaman.	Amount Paid.	Remarks.
				$ cts.	
HANTS—(*Con.*)	Newport	3430	Harvey, Robert.		Services not proved.
	do	3431	Harvey, Berjamin		do
	Noel	3356	Whitear, Isaac		do
	Rawdon	3305	Knowl 3, William		do
	do	3370	Smith, John		do
	do	3369	Haines, Robert		do
	do	3368	Wire, George		do
	Shubenacadie	3380	Miller, George		do
	do	3425	Blois, John		do
	Ste. Croix	3437	Bates, Thomas		do
KINGS	do	3429	Hunter, James		do
	Windsor	3436	Allison, Matthew.		do
	do	3455	Redden, Joseph		do
LUNENBURG	Avonport	3444	Vulley, John		do
PICTOU	Grafton	3502	Cushing, Robert		do
RICHMOND	Hall's Harbour	3450	Martin, Samuel		do
	Lunenburg	3221	Kinckle, John Fred	20 00	
	River John	2842	Shea, William	20 00	
	West Arichat	2813	Picard, Jean B.	20 00	

PENSIONS TO MILITIAMEN OF 1812-15.—*Continued.*

PROVINCE OF MANITOBA.

Electoral District.	Post Office.	Number of Cases.	Name of Militiaman.	Amount Paid.	Remarks.
				$ cts.	
MARQUETTE	Baie St. Paul	2530	Delorme, Jean B.		Dead.
	St.François Xavier	2342	Bonamy-Lespérance, Alexis	20 00	
	do	2333	Lepine, Jean B.		Dead.
LISGAR	St. Paul	219	Markeley, Christopher	20 00	
SELKIRK	St. Boniface	3112	Charbonneau, Jean B.	20 00	

PENSIONS TO MILITIAMEN OF 1812-15.—*Continued.*

PROVINCE OF PRINCE EDWARD ISLAND.

Electoral District.	Post Office.	Number of Case.	Name of Militiaman.	Amount Paid.	Remarks.
				$ cts.	
PRINCE	Campbellton	3396	Wall, Daniel		Services not proved.
	Malpec	3394	Matthews, Alexander.....	....	do
	St. Eleonors..........	3405	McKay, Archibald........	....	do

RÉSUMÉ.

Province.	Total Number of Cases.	Cases in Abeyance.	Action.				Amount Paid.
			Disallowed.		No Return.	Cases Paid.	
			Dead.	Left Limits.			
							$ cts.
Ontario	1108	60	86	5	33	924	18,180 00
Quebec	1695	70	155	4	27	1439	29,780 00
New Brunswick............	37	4	3	0	2	29	530 00
Nova Scotia....	77	60	0	0	0	17	340 00
Prince Edward Island....	3	3	0	0	0	0	....
Manitoba	5	0	2	0	0	3	60 00
Totals.........	2925	197	246	9	62	2412	48,240 00

Paid Balance of Claims, 1875-6........	1,760 00
Total Amount voted, 1876-7	50,000 00

C. E. PANET, L.C.,
Deputy of the Minister of Militia and Defense.

OTTAWA, 1877.

www.ingramcontent.com/pod-product-compliance
Lightning Source LLC
Chambersburg PA
CBHW030542270326
41927CB00008B/1475